MW00423377

"Unlock the key to credibility digital self-doubt again! Don't Make it weird is exactly what every entrepreneur needs to walk away from transactional interactions and toward genuine connections that drive business."

—KATHERINE WINTSCH,
the author of *Slay Like a Mother*

"Imagine you have a friend who has built a multi-million dollar business successfully (and authentically) leveraging social media as an entrepreneur. Now imagine this friend generously shares with you all her tips, tricks, wisdom and strategies in ways that are actionable, effective AND make you belly laugh because, oh, by the way, she's also hilarious. That's Colleen Nichols and *Don't Make It Weird* in a nutshell."

—ALLIE REEVES,
Business Mentor and Host of the Top Rated Business Podcast *All in with Allie*

"Colleen has this amazing and rare gift of being able to be brutally honest, vulnerable, authentic, hilarious and inspiring... all at the same time. What's even more impressive is that she's able to pull those same qualities out of others and give them a chance at experiencing the joy and freedom that comes from truly being themselves online. As her friend, I'm so proud and as a fellow entrepreneur, I'm incredibly inspired. This book is going to be a catalyst for so many to step into who they were always called to be as entrepreneurs and I'm here for it!! "

—KATELYN JAMES,
CEO and Digital Course Creator

"Colleen's No-B.S. approach is gold. She doesn't just tell you how to be yourself online; she *teaches* you. This is more than a book, it's your workbook, it's your journal, it's your guide for building a successful brand and online business."

—ANNALIESE WEGNER,
Advocate for Agriculture, Speaker + Digital Creator

The Entrepreneur's Guide to
Being Human on the Internet

DON'T MAKE IT WEIRD

COLLEEN NICHOLS

Fedd Books
P.O. Box 341973
Austin, TX 78734

www.thefeddagency.com

Published in association with The Fedd Agency, Inc., a literary agency.

ISBN: 978-1-957616-53-7
eISBN: 978-1-957616-54-4

LCCN: 2023918957

Printed in the United States of America

TABLE OF CONTENTS

DEDICATION

To my mom, for making me the human I am today.

To Cory, for always, without fail, loving the human that I am.

FOREWORD

By Shauna Vanbogart

When Colleen Nichols asked me to write the foreword for her book, I was simultaneously flattered and incredibly confused.

Me? The woman who has gone MIA on social media for months now?

Me? The seasoned business owner who still—embarrassingly—has no idea what she's doing on social media and seems to feel more confused (and old) as the days pass?

If there's an unspoken customer avatar for her book, *Don't Make It Weird*, it's definitely me. I am the queen of overthinking my online persona. If you even knew the amount of insecure text messages I've sent Colleen asking her to review something I've posted or desperately asking, "Should I delete it?" you'd know the book title alone is a statement explicitly directed at me.

Even Colleen's delightful husband remarked about me after taking our online relationship to a face-to-face, joint family vacation. "She's way cooler in person than I thought she'd be." (Thank you, Cory! And

I agree—where exactly does my cool go when I open Instagram to make a post?).

The further irony of being asked to write a foreword for a book on how to be a captivating human on the internet (and make money doing so), is that my entire research thesis for my graduate degree, for which I was published in 2013, centered around building credibility online.

At the time, I ran a full-service image consulting firm, showing individuals how to leverage their built-in tools of appearance, behavior, communication, and personality to achieve success in their life (more sales, more clients, better relationships, etc.). Professionals who were previously generating business from face-to-face networking events and BNI (if you don't know what BNI is, we likely have a different skincare regimen), were now learning to navigate a new, shiny online space where professional headshots were becoming increasingly important, and Facebook was the go-to microphone to sell your services and products.

A core finding of my research was how the act of self-disclosure—conveying personal information about yourself—was a necessary component of building trust, likability, and thus, credibility, among an intended audience.

Without sprinkling in parts of their non-business life, whether it be their family, the garden they love tending to in the backyard, or the meal they cooked from scratch, business owners became transactional, overly curated robots that people couldn't connect with. And without connection, the necessary foundation of trust for potential clients to easily hit the buy button on their website didn't exist.

The major thought leaders of that time who had amassed an incredible amount of success online were consistently using self-disclosure as a tactic to build trust. You'd find personal photos on their website "about" pages and behind-the-scenes snapshots shared to their Facebook feed (this was pre-Instagram).

This was a fascinating discovery in my research and was a clear, yet totally overlooked, differentiator between those who were successful and those who were struggling. Everyone at that time wanted to be the next Marie Forleo, and everyone started mimicking what they thought were the special ingredients to having a similar kind of success. I can only imagine the amount of cease-and-desist letters that went out from the Marie Forleo empire.

But what most people overlooked was the secret sauce—the ability to harness one's uniqueness and translate it online in a way that didn't feel watered down or overthought so that they could create immediate trust with their audience (and thus a shorter sales cycle). Instead, people fixated on branding, fonts, and funnels, convincing themselves that having the right bullet points on their website copy would finally be the thing that quantum leaped them into a multi-six-figure business.

Then there are people like Colleen. I want to say she's a rare find (and she is, to me) but that would insinuate you've got to have something special about you to make the wisdom of her book pay off (and you absolutely do not).

Colleen is not only a spectacular example of effective and authentic self-disclosure, she's completely leveled-up the experience by mastering genuine connection with her audience. She has an innate skill to make anyone in her presence feel seen, heard, and accepted without getting lost in their lane or placating them to be liked. She's herself, and she lets you be you. What you see online is what you get in person. Everything she has written in this book validates and builds upon the research I discovered over a decade ago—being human is an essential part of the equation.

She's not thinking about how to be genuine; she just is. Yet, there's strategy involved. She plays the game of business but keeps her authenticity intact as she does it. What she emulates is the secret sauce we've all been after.

You're hard-pressed to find people who excel at something and can also teach it. *Don't Make It Weird* is a valuable road map that doesn't feel overly complicated or manipulative (far from it). This is a manual for being you in the necessary way that your online business requires it if success is what you're after. And how she leads you there may surprise you. You've come for a social media strategy but stay open for the inevitable breakthroughs in other departments of your life.

You'll feel like she's right there on the couch with you as you read, prompting you to reflect on the questions she poses. If you treat this as a prescription for overthinking your online presence, you'll find your remedy by showing up to the entire experience—the reflection questions, the journal prompts, and especially the fourteen-day Consistency Calculation at the end. There's no extra fluff here, I promise. Because I sat my butt down and read the very book I needed the most at this point in my career. And when people ask me what contributed to my success in 2023, you better believe I'll be telling them, "I finally stopped making it weird."

LET'S GET SOME THINGS STRAIGHT

I didn't want to write a book.

Everyone who's written a book says that once you do, you become an authority on the topic you've spent hours of your life researching (and, in my case, *years* gabbing about on social media). They say that people will be more willing to listen to you, interview you, and hire you when you write a book, and that's scary. I have this terrifying goal that one day I'll be on TV or on big stages talking about business and social media and the psychology behind it all, but part of me cringes at the thought, because I'm not a guru, and I have a real struggle with authority figures (so how could I possibly *become* one?!). I'm filled with anxiety and self-doubt, and I often feel like I have no idea what I'm doing. Imposter syndrome is a close friend of mine, and we hang out together often. I regularly feel like I don't have my shit together. But then again, doesn't everyone feel that way? (This is a rhetorical question; please don't @ me if you are the rare unicorn who has her shit together.)

I decided to write this book for you, my fellow normal human who is also trying to do all the things, all the time, and constantly thwarting the ever-present buzz in the back of your mind that sounds a hell of a lot like *Am I even doing this right?* I'm writing this because I was once a little girl who sat in her room for hours on end, writing her thoughts and feelings and made-up stories in the pages of countless notebooks (some of which are sitting next to me right now as encouragement for when I want to pull the plug on this project). I'm writing it because I've accomplished things that I couldn't have even conceived in my wildest dreams, and I've been able to stay true to myself throughout the entire process. I'm writing this because I want to prove to you that *you* can achieve whatever it is that feels like success and abundance to you, too. You can take a deep breath because I'm not going to tell you that you need to become a carbon copy of me and do every little thing I've done over the past ten years (because then *you'd* need more therapy). I'm not going to tell you that you need to understand the inner workings of the algorithm or regard me as the be-all and end-all (because that would be laughable).

> I'm also not going to shove sunshine up your ass in hopes of creating rainbow burps. This isn't rocket science; it's common sense.

I'm also not going to shove sunshine up your ass in hopes of creating rainbow burps. This isn't rocket science; it's common sense (but as my grandfather always said, "Common sense is not common," and boy howdy, I think he's rolling over in his grave as I try to write a book about it).

Everything I'm going to walk you through is going to lead you to the most important tool for your business: *the real you.* I'm not promising you that you'll love every part of the process, but I'm confident that if you stick with it, you'll find that it'll be worth it. So let's go dig through the bullshit that's holding you back, shall we? It's time for you to become a magnetic human on the internet without *making it weird.*

Chapter 01

RIPPING UP
THE MOTIVATIONAL
CAT POSTERS

Once upon a time, there was a world where business owners and entrepreneurs thrived in brick-and-mortar stores, networking happy hour events, and face-to-face meetings. They gleefully handed out business cards and used WordArt to create sales PowerPoints. It was a time when marketing budgets were primarily allocated to radio ads and TV commercials, and sales were closed by men on golf courses and not women in DMs. Alas, that world is long gone, and we now exist in the land of endless possibilities, *literally* in the palm of your hand. Today, anyone with a phone and WIFI has the ability to create a stream of income, but many people are left fumbling the ball when it comes to how they use one of the most critical business tools in today's world: social media.

After spending nearly a decade building a brand and multiple businesses from my comfy corner of the internet, it became clear that I was doing things in a way that was different from most people. I would often get asked about my successes, and I was dumbfounded because I truly couldn't see the answer. My brain does this super inconvenient thing where it tells me if I'm capable of doing something, it has to be so outrageously simple that literally anyone else could do it in their sleep (and yes, I do need more therapy).

The truth is, I'm not better than anyone.

I'm not an expert in SEO.

I don't have a hashtag strategy.

I couldn't make a pretty graphic in Canva to save my life.

I didn't go to business school.

I can barely add or subtract without using my fingers.

I don't believe in luck, but I don't know any other way to explain how or why certain TikToks and Reels go viral.

I didn't grow up in a family with extra money.

I have a diagnosed anxiety disorder that I'm absolutely medicated for.

I don't have a hidden talent.

I don't have a morning routine, I'm inconsistent at best when it comes to working out, and I like to eat dessert every night.

I'm painfully average.

Despite all that, I've made millions of dollars building businesses solely on social media . . . without ever running an ad or paying to promote posts.

How? I've spent the last decade perfecting the art of being human on the internet, blending authenticity and strategy in such a way that it's often difficult for my community to separate the two. That, my new friend, is why people connect and spend their money with me—and I'm going to teach you exactly how to do it, too.

SWALLOWING THE HARD PILL

First things first: I'm not going to change your life, and neither is this book. You can read all the personal development books, listen to all the podcasts, and journal your way into oblivion, but all of that will be a waste of time and money if you don't create discipline within yourself and your business.

For the vast majority of the time, working for yourself in any capacity is less than glamorous, and it's hard as hell. When you work for yourself, you don't have a manager making sure you're completing tasks that check the boxes of your job description. You don't have the pressure of knowing your boss sees when you clock in and clock out, or how often you wiggle your mouse during your work from home days. No one is there to make sure you get your ass to work every day. And honestly, no one cares (besides you, of course).

As an entrepreneur, it's easy to get sucked into the self-help spiral. We all think one more book, one more course, or one more coach will help us uncover the motivation somewhere within ourselves that will help propel us beyond our wildest dreams.

Sure, books and courses and coaches can absolutely act as the catalysts to the level of success so many of us long to discover, but in the end, *you're* the secret sauce that's going to determine if that other stuff was even worth it. Have you ever invested in a course or coach, only to check out halfway through the process? I sure as hell have. Either it was too uncomfortable, or life got too *lifey*, and I did what felt most natural to me: I fell off track. It wasn't the coach or the course's fault, though. It was mine. This may or may not be the best book you've ever read, but I'm confident you're going to get exactly what you need from it. What's meant for you will find you, and you can leave the rest. But go ahead and make a promise to yourself right here and now that you're going to take radical responsibility for whatever happens next. Only you can make or break your business. I'm here to hold up a mirror, offer some ideas, and do my best to set your metaphorical car on the right track, but ultimately, it's you who decides whether or not you're going to *actually* go anywhere.

While we're sitting here talking about radical responsibility, can we make another deal right here and right now that we'll all stop telling ourselves that we need to be "more motivated" to succeed? My God, if I see one more motivational boss babe quote making its way into your Stories, I'll cut a bitch. Not because I dislike the idea of you being motivated. I dislike the idea of you beating yourself up over not having enough of it. You're wasting your energy trying to multiply the wrong resource.

According to a quick Google search, motivation can be defined as the general desire or willingness to do something. Motivation will get you to *start* your business. It'll light that fire under your happy ass to create the Instagram account or pick your branding colors, because that shit is *fun*. We all desire and are willing to have fun. But you're in for a rude awakening if you think building a brand and business that results in a significant chunk of change is always fun.

There are going to be days when you're tired, void of even an ounce of creativity, or when the only desire you'll have is to burn it all down and walk away.

That's when motivation is on vacation somewhere on a tropical island and you're waking up in reality town all alone. When those days come, which they absolutely will, you're going to need discipline in your back pocket (or, honestly, the driver's seat).

So says my OG business coach, Google, discipline is the ability to train oneself to do something in a controlled and habitual way. Discipline is what's going to be there to pick you up off the floor when motivation is dancing in the rain with her new Latin lover. Discipline is going to carry you to write the content, show up, and deliver when motivation is taking an afternoon catnap.

Truth be told, I've built a multimillion-dollar business in the last fifteen months, and I am rarely motivated. If it were up to my motivation, I'd be taking a nap right now with my toddler rather than sitting here in my office writing this book.

The real resource you need to tap into is discipline, because *discipline* is what's going to create the results you desire. As our world continues to make the transition from always in-person to mostly online, it's critical that you know how to take your humanness and be able to seamlessly translate it from in-person to online. Showing up in ways that you're not used to, or even comfortable with, is going to feel like a struggle at times, and simply being motivated to learn how to do this isn't going to cut it. You need to create a sense of discipline in your life and your business that automatically kicks in when your motivation goes AWOL.

> It's critical that you know how to take your humanness and be able to seamlessly translate it from in-person to online.

DON'T MAKE IT WEIRD

DON'T MAKE IT WEIRD

HERE'S THE PART WHERE YOU ACTUALLY DO SOMETHING

You didn't think I'd just let this be a passive experience for you, did you? Listen, I'm all about journaling—it's how some of my best ideas come to light (and some of my biggest frustrations are brought to the surface for me to examine). Either you love it, too, or it feels clunky and awkward. (There's really no in between is there?) Even if it's not your thing to sit down and journal, can you at least maybe kinda sorta try? It really doesn't have to be pretty or long-winded or life-altering. It's simply meant to act as a way to get you out of your own damn head. Maybe it's easier to do in the notes section on your phone, or in a voice recording, or by simply talking out loud to yourself (don't knock it 'til you've tried it), or by making a list of bullet points. I don't care *how* it looks; I only care that you try. Capisce? (And yes, that is absolutely an Uncle Jesse *Full House* reference. You're welcome/I'm sorry.) Take a look at these prompts and work your way through them. Remember, there is no right or wrong way to do this shit. Just try, okay?

6

In what areas of your life are you disciplined AF? How does it serve you? For me, it's my work. I have a rock-solid sense of discipline in this area of my life, and it serves me well financially and emotionally and gives me a sense of purpose. I'm proud of myself, and I like that feeling.

Your turn. In what areas of your life are you disciplined AF? How does it serve you?

In what areas of your life are you lacking in the discipline department? How does it affect you? Um, for me, it can all fall under the health and wellness umbrella. Some weeks I'm *gung ho* about eating twenty-seven veggies a day, and then some weeks I'm all about baked goods. It acts as a hindrance because I constantly feel like I'm start/stopping all over the place, and the lack of consistency makes it feel impossible to achieve any real results that I'm looking (but not working) for.

Your turn. In what areas of your life are you lacking in the discipline department? How does it affect you?

What does motivation look and feel like for you? While motivation alone will rarely be the thing that gets you across the finish line, it is important and wonderful to embrace. For example, I feel motivated by talking about business and brainstorming new ideas, offerings, and content (both for myself and my friends!). Those types of conversations truly light a fire underneath me and make me feel like I could pull a Kool-Aid Man situation and bust through a brick wall.

Your turn. What does motivation look and feel like for you?

How often do you partake in activities that feed your motivation?
For example, there are times that I'm so in the zone—work, work,
working—when I start feeling myself fading fast. When that feeling
creeps up on me, I'll call one of my entrepreneurial friends and ask if
she wants to grab coffee so we can chat about what's going on in our
business worlds.

    **Your turn. How often do you partake in activities that feed your
motivation?**

_____

_____

_____

_____

_____

_____

_____

_____

_____

_____

If I could wave a magic wand and, by the end of this book, something in your life could change, what would it be? What would it look (and feel) like? To be clear, I have no magic wand, but this question is a powerful one—because your answer will reveal so much about you and your journey.

Your turn. I'm waving my pretend magic wand, and by the end of this book, something in your life will change. What would it be? What would it look (and feel) like?

_____

_____

_____

_____

_____

_____

_____

_____

_____

Chapter 02

FROM PEDESTAL TO DUMPSTER FIRE

Right before I dove headfirst into my entrepreneurial journey in January 2017, my life had turned into a complete dumpster fire. Not only was my master's degree in mental health counseling collecting dust in the attic while I was the Head Snack Bitch in Charge for my toddler and nursing a newborn seemingly 24/7, but my husband (and sole income earner) had recently lost his job out of the blue.

My husband losing his job was one of those moments that created a clear divide in my life. The divide between sitting high atop a pedestal that you unknowingly set yourself on, and life throwing a curveball, shattering it to the ground. There was The Before and The After. I'm almost embarrassed to admit how I viewed life during The Before. Honest to God, I thought I had made it. I lived in a house where I got to select things like the granite countertop in the kitchen and the bathroom shower tile. I lived in a neighborhood with *sidewalks*, people. And my bedroom had two walk-in closets. I grew up with a mom who worked multiple jobs at once so we could have what we <u>needed</u>, and I was living a life where my husband made enough money for me to be a stay-at-home-mom (that's some rich people shit, okay?). Never mind that we still lived paycheck to paycheck, had no real savings, and my husband's job was a soul-sucking vacuum; the trappings were there, and we were more "successful" than I could have ever imagined. When The After line was drawn in the sand, I was six months pregnant and had just waddled my way to the couch after putting my sixteen-month-old down for a nap. *Sweet silence*, I remember thinking to myself. My biggest concern in that moment was whether I should lay right down and take a nap or continue binge-watching *Pretty Little Liars*. Before I could even make up my mind, I got a text from my husband, Cory.

"Just got fired."

"WHO just got fired?" I hurriedly texted back, all but grabbing the popcorn.

Cory was a VP at the company, so surely he was talking about a certain employee that he had been bitching about for the past several months.

When he didn't answer me, I called him.

"Who got fired?" I asked.

In one breath, he said, "I did. I'll call you back." Click.

That's when the room started to do that thing where it spins and you're not quite sure if you're having a panic attack or dying.

I vividly remember sitting in the corner of our gray sectional, looking around at my living room in the dream house we had built a few years prior. Growing up as a kid who didn't have a fancy house or a family with money, and as the first person in my immediate family to graduate from college, this house was my stamp of "I've made it." When I moved into that house, I also moved myself onto a pedestal, and one phone call knocked me the fuck off.

Questions drenched in panic immediately began running through my head.

How will we pay our mortgage? No one is going to hire a six-months-pregnant woman.

Will we have insurance when the baby gets here? Or are we giving a new meaning to "a million-dollar baby"?

How will we afford a car? I'm going out on a limb here and assuming the company car that Cory drove won't be coming home with him.

The room just kept spinning. With tears running down my face, I woke my toddler up from his nap (which, if you're a parent who has a kid that sucks at napping, you know that waking my sleeping baby was almost as painful as the unemployment news) and went to pick up Cory. It was like a scene out of a movie; he was standing there outside of the office building holding a brown box full of picture frames and other trinkets from his office. To my shock and disbelief (and mild frustration), Cory wasn't nearly as upset as I was—he looked *lighter*. His face was calm. It was clear that he understood the gravity of the situation, but he was *relieved* to be cut loose from the golden handcuffs of that job. Cory ended up getting a small severance that floated us for a few months, and thus started what we refer to as "Severance Summer."

We got a taste of what it was like to not have Cory in a toxic work environment. I didn't realize I had lost a piece of my husband, but it was obvious when I started getting him back. His sense of humor thawed, conversations didn't revolve around things that were pissing him off, and he was *fun* again. We liked the way we could both spend time with our son during the day, and that we didn't have to cram the ideal "family time" portion of our life into just Saturday and Sunday. We liked that we could create a schedule that worked for us. Cory liked not having to be out the door by 6:30 a.m., and I liked having a little extra help with the baby in the morning. It was as if the rug had been pulled out from under us, but the curtain was pulled back at the same time. We were beginning to see how life as we knew it *could* feel different. We knew it wouldn't be a pleasure cruise, but that's when we decided we'd do everything in our power to never work in a traditional setting ever again.

Here comes the unsexy part about discipline that doesn't feel awesome but pays off in the long run. The time of dipping my toe into the entrepreneurial pool was when the dust of The After was settling and I could comprehend my new reality. I had a twenty-month-old and a four-week-old, and we were selling our dream home because we couldn't afford the mortgage anymore. We downsized from the beautiful 3,200-square-foot house that we built, to an 1,800-square-foot home that was thirty years old, had blue carpet upstairs, and outdated tile flooring in the kitchen (neither of which we could afford to replace). To call that period of my life "humbling" would be the understatement of the century. It felt like a backslide into the life that I had desperately tried to uplevel from, and I would go

> It was as if the rug had been pulled out from under us, but the curtain was pulled back at the same time. We were beginning to see how life as we knew it *could* feel different.

on to spend the next five years grinding to make sure we didn't stay there. Enter: me, trying to make money from home using social media. The only time I had to actually sit down and get business-related work done was after my kids went to bed. This is probably something I should dig deeper into with my therapist, but what I like doing at the end of the day is sitting down and watching true crime shows. I mean, what doesn't calm the nervous system like watching a story about someone else getting abducted and murdered, am I right? I digress.

After the boys were in bed, I had two options. I could sit my tired ass on the couch and watch a two-hour-long true crime documentary, or I could do something that would actually help me make a change in our less-than-ideal reality. So for the first eighteen months of my business, I completely gave up TV. If I had time to watch TV, that meant I had time to get my business off the ground, and I chose liftoff.

HERE'S THE PART WHERE YOU ACTUALLY DO SOMETHING

Riddle me this, my friend: What does "liftoff" look like for you? This is different for everyone, and it's something that evolves over time. Like I said, for me in 2017, liftoff was finding a way to get myself out there and start making enough money to help with groceries, and that is one of the most powerful fires that has ever been lit underneath me. The humblest of desires can lead to the most life-altering outcomes.

What is something you can change right now (like, tuh-day) that would get you one step closer to your dream? For me, it was turning off the damn TV and taking action. That's it. Don't overcomplicate this one, Becky.

Chapter 03

YOUR GPS MIGHT BE LYING TO YOU

Social media is ripe with "anti-hustle" culture, but I want to remind you that working hard isn't toxic. Working hard is *necessary* to rise to the top. Making sacrifices and choosing to put your future desires ahead of your current wants is a baseline requirement when you're trying to build a business. But you have to understand that it's seasonal. It won't (or at least *shouldn't*) always be that way. Do I watch TV now? You bet your sweet ass I do. But even still, after growing a successful business, I sometimes struggle with sitting down and doing nothing in the evenings. The reason I sit down, relax, and do "nothing" is because I *know* the importance of rest (which we'll talk about later, but for now we're focusing on getting your ass in gear). I understand how critical it is to *not* always be "on." But in the beginning, or

> Making sacrifices and choosing to put your future desires ahead of your current wants is a baseline requirement when you're trying to build a business.

when you're trying to bring about massive growth and expansion, you'll often be leaning on discipline to get you there.

HERE'S THE PART WHERE YOU ACTUALLY DO SOMETHING

To help you create that sense of discipline in your life and business, I want you to journal a few questions. Note: when I say *journal*, I mean *freewrite*. This is not the time to care about how neat your handwriting is, if you spelled *entrepreneur* correctly, or if your dreams and desires sound "realistic." (I hope they don't, actually.) It's about creating a space where you can be completely open and honest with yourself, because when you do that, monumental shifts will occur.

1. What will the outcome be if I *choose* to *not* make my business a non-negotiable?
   a. How will that feel?
   b. Who will be affected?
   c. What pain/discomfort/frustration will I be continuing to choose?

2. What will the outcome be if I DO *choose* to make my business a non-negotiable?
   a. How will that feel?
   b. What will I have?
   c. Who will be affected?
   d. What pain/discomfort/frustration would be alleviated? What would it be replaced with?

WHEN TO USE A ROAD MAP

The question we want to start with, though, is, "Where are you trying to get to?" At the risk of sounding like a motivational cat poster that many elder millennials like me remember from our grade school classrooms, so much of entrepreneurship is about the journey. (Trust me, I gagged just typing that, but damn it, it's true.) I think about it like a road trip. For the past several years, my husband and I have packed our family into the car and made the twelve-hour road trip from Richmond, Virginia, to Cape Cod, Massachusetts, to spend a week with some of our dearest friends. Much like being an entrepreneur, embarking on a road trip with kids can feel like a special place in hell if you fail to plan correctly.

When we make our voyage to Cape Cod, we start prepping the car days in advance. We make sure we get an oil change, fill up the tank with gas, get the iPad holder thing set up so the boys have movies to watch (which, of course, I have to plan ahead and download before we leave), and we research what true crime podcasts we want to binge. I even make a special grocery store trip *just* for the car snacks. We decide which route we're going to take, and plan where we'll stop for lunch along the way. (Food is a critical part of my road trip experience, okay?)

Even though we've been together for nearly twenty years, my favorite part of long car rides are the conversations with Cory. We talk about life and business and everything in between, and oftentimes we don't turn on any music or podcasts until hours into the drive. It's a time where we're without our normal distractions (or they're strapped down in the back), and we have time to just talk. Are there detours and traffic jams along the way? Sure. That's to be expected, but when we pull onto the Cape, we're able to roll the windows down to smell the ocean and enjoy the reward of all that planning and effort it took to get there.

Now imagine if we tried to make that same trip without knowing where we were headed. What would that experience look like if our friends told us, "Come on vacation with us!" but didn't tell us *where* that vacation was going to take place? Even if they told us to drive to New England, we absolutely *could* do that, but it's highly unlikely we would end up with them at the right house on Cape Cod. We'd end up wasting time, energy, and resources wandering up north, not exactly sure where we were headed.

Your business is no different. I understand you want to be an entrepreneur, a CEO, or an influencer, but what are the details of what you actually want to accomplish while on that journey of becoming? Just like it would be an epic waste of time, energy, and resources if we tried to go on a road trip without our final destination clearly in mind, it will feel like the same result if you don't understand where you want this journey to take you.

Now, where you want the journey to take you may very well change along the way. When I started up a network marketing side gig, the "end game" for me was the ability to make $500 a month to help with groceries. At that point in time, *grocery money* was as far as I could see on my journey. When I quickly earned more than that, I adjusted the scope of my journey to take me to a place where I could cover groceries *and* our mortgage every month. At that time, I still very much considered myself to be a full-time stay-at-home mom, so it felt like a major accomplishment to be able to financially contribute in that way. My point in telling you this is that if I had originally said, "I want to build my own multimillion-dollar business, grow an Instagram account to over 140,000 followers, be an author, and get paid for speaking at events," it wouldn't have registered with me because it wouldn't have been a journey that I even wanted to embark upon. So when I tell you that you need to know where you want this journey to take you, I need you to know the first leg of your trip—not the detailed itinerary of what you'll do when you arrive. Every time you arrive at the intended destination, the next part of the journey will reveal itself. Just like when we get to Cape Cod, it doesn't mean we're staying still. One day we'll take a day trip to Provincetown, another day we'll go whale watching, and another day we'll spend hours at the bay while our boys play in the sand and eat an ungodly amount of Goldfish and pretzels. You need to worry about the *what* of the matter and leave the *how* up to the Universe (or HaShem, or whatever you want to call it).

WHEN THE ROAD MAP DOESN'T FUCKING MATTER

Okay, so we've built a case for why and when having a road map might actually matter. You know, when it's necessary to have a clear understanding of where you're headed. Point being, you can't just say, "I want to be an entrepreneur," and then hop into the proverbial car and set out on your business-building journey. That's a cute idea, Brittany, but it's going to be an even rougher road than necessary if you don't know what kind of entrepreneurial journey you're taking.

For example, my friend Kasey is a successful entrepreneur who uses her background in psychology to train her clients. I, too, am a successful entrepreneur who uses my background in psychology to train my clients, but I didn't use Kasey's road map. Kasey's services are locally based; mine are not. Kasey holds in-person classes; I do not. Kasey is contracted by clients, typically, for four to six weeks, while my membership community is a twelve-month-long commitment. Kasey invests in radio ads; I live on Instagram. Oh! I almost forgot: Kasey's clients are *dogs*, and mine are *humans*. If I said to myself and the Universe, "I want to use my background in psychology to train clients," and then ended up in a room full of dogs, I'd be shit outta luck.

Had I followed Kasey's business road map, or she mine, neither of us would have built the level of success we currently enjoy. But what about when you're working with the same population (i.e., *humans*) as someone else who is more successful than you? Wouldn't it make sense to try to emulate them?

Not always.

When I was in graduate school, blogs were a big thing, and there were half a dozen or so that I regularly read. Julie was the author of one, and Courtney authored another. I loved reading their posts about their days, or their favorite recipe from the week, or a new circuit workout they had been loving. I also thought it was so freaking cool that they got paid for certain posts and were sent free products from companies, and after a while, I found other blogs that fell under the "healthy living blog" umbrella. The more I read, the more I thought, "I'm as good of a writer as any of them. . . . I should start my *own* healthy living blog."

Never mind the fact that healthy living wasn't exactly my way of life, unless, of course, you consider fighting with body dysmorphia and disordered eating *healthy living*. So, I started a blog with no idea what I was doing other than trying to emulate Julie and Courtney. I structured my posts like they did (even though I didn't have to do that). I took pictures of my food like they did (tastefully omitting the fact that I hate cooking). I wrote about workouts I did (all while leaving out the parts about doing them out of self-guilt and shame). I enjoyed it, and I was gaining some traction, but not to the level that I knew was possible.

Then the day came when I was going to write about making a healthy dinner; I had found a new recipe that I was excited to try, and when Cory walked into the kitchen to find me at the sink peeling a vegetable, he asked what we were having.

"It's a chicken and zucchini dish," I answered.

To which he replied, "Then why are you peeling those cucumbers?"

Initially, I felt like a big fat idiot, but ultimately, I remember laughing until we cried. I also remember that we ended up going to Chipotle because the dish really wasn't going to work with those *cucumbers*. That night, I wrote a post and titled it "DOHmestic Diva," sewn together with self-deprecation, humor, and a lesson in learning to laugh at yourself. And waddyaknow? It got the most engagement I'd ever received on a post. It was shared multiple times on Facebook for the first time ever, and I had comments from *strangers!* I couldn't believe that people other than my mom and Cory were actually reading (and laughing at) the words I wrote.

After that post, I quickly discovered and developed my writing style and tone of voice (which is casual; I write the same way that I speak), and things started to take off. I was regularly getting paid to post on my blog, I was routinely working with different brands outside of the "healthy living" genre, and I was creating a community of readers, many of whom are still friends and followers of mine on social media. (They've stuck with me for over a decade, and that absolutely blows my mind.)

As you can see, this is an example of when the road map wasn't necessarily helpful. I knew what I wanted to do (write a blog), but when I used someone else's road map, it didn't take me to the destination I was aiming for. It was only when I started trusting myself and my inner compass that I was able to find myself on the right track. So if you're currently in business and you feel stuck despite showing up and doing the damn thing, I encourage you to pay attention to whose road map you're using. While there are absolutely times when it's appropriate (and just plain smart) to use someone else's road map, there are certainly times when it's better to turn off the GPS, go for a joy ride, and see where you end up.

Another great example of this is my friend, Sara. She came into my orbit when I launched Direct Sales Growth Community (my membership platform—DSGC), and she was the epitome of an eager beaver. She had big goals, and she was willing to do whatever it took to accomplish them. Then came the rub of her not agreeing with a training of mine. I trained on how I did reach-outs in the beginning of my business in a human, non-icky way, and that I considered reach-outs to be a critical part of growing your business quickly. The way I train people to do sales reach-outs has a proven track record, but Sara wanted nothing to do with it. No matter the context, reach-outs felt gross to her—it was part of my road map that didn't fit her journey.

Because Sara has totally mastered the art of knowing herself, she took what she needed from me, but ultimately trusted herself and used her inner compass for her journey. She started showing up double time in her Instagram Stories, having authentic conversations that transformed her followers into a community, and her business exploded. Not only were her personal sales growing, but she also started building a massive organization. She took it a step further over a year later when she felt the nudge to pivot her business. On paper, it might not have made sense; she had a good thing going, and making a move to start over was not only risky, but it was also scary as hell. I remember her texting me and telling me about the decision she was pondering, and she asked for my advice. Obviously, I don't remember verbatim what I said, but I know the gist was that she knew what the right answer was, and that if she could take just even a few minutes and remove the fear from the situation, she'd see it. The next day, she made the pivot, and everything immediately clicked into place. She was more than doubling her previous sales, her team grew to over 100 people in less than a week, and she finally started seeing how this "side gig" could morph into a "full-time income." And from the outside looking in, it was like watching a person glow from the inside out. Her light was shining at a capacity I hadn't seen before, and it was clearly a magnet for success and sales.

Had Sara used my exact entrepreneurial road map, this wouldn't have been the result. If she had tried to emulate my exact journey, it would have been met with inner force and frustration, and ultimately that would have led to burnout and/or giving up. There are few things more powerful in your entrepreneurial life than knowing when to take direction from someone else, or when it's time to look inward and trust yourself more than anything or anyone else. If you've surrounded yourself with quality mentors and coaches, they'll be guiding you towards that destination every single time.

MIMETIC DESIRE: WANTING IT BECAUSE SOMEONE ELSE WANTED IT FIRST

While we talk about why it's important to understand where you're going, it's equally important to understand *why* you want to go there in the first place.

Since we're friends now, I have no problem being honest and admitting to you that I'm someone who is in active recovery from an achievement addiction. If there are any other Enneagram 3s reading this book, you know exactly what I'm talkin' about. Failing (meaning, not achieving my goals *exactly* when and how I planned) often feels like a fate worse than death, and achieving anything that comes along with praise and recognition is my motherfucking drug of choice.

The thing is, I wouldn't consider myself to be a competitive person, which has always left me with a slight identity crisis. I want to be the best, but I don't want to have to compete for it. Good golly, Miss Molly, there is nothing that shuts me down faster than an actual competition. While there's rarely a time that I don't have something I'm trying to achieve, as soon as it becomes a race with someone or something outside of myself, I'll bow out, because winning against someone else doesn't give me the same satisfaction as accomplishing whatever it is I set out to do. That used to make me feel like a pushover, or someone who was incapable of winning, because unlike my brother, who loved participating in everything from organized sports to family game night, I was repelled by all of it. The thought of losing, of not being the best, or of simply looking dumb was *so paralyzing* to me that I'd do anything in my power to avoid it. Even well into adulthood, I assumed the role of someone who wasn't capable of achieving any kind of real success because I'd eventually have to compete with someone to "win." That was the only type of success I considered possible, and it wasn't until a random therapy session that I realized that my definition of success had been built solely on other people's definitions of "winning," even though I'd been given contrary examples my entire life.

All throughout grade school, PE class was the bane of my existence. I have the athletic ability of a fruit fly, and PE class gave me ample opportunity to face death, a.k.a. publicly not being the best. The capstone of every semester in PE was the class where we had to run the mile. I would have crippling anxiety on the days leading up to it, and I would do my best to manifest the plague, a broken leg, or even *my first period*—anything to hopefully get me out of that dreadful day. This had been my pattern for years, and finally my mom had had enough of my bullshit (and honestly, as a mom now myself, I don't blame her one bit). She used my greatest mental roadblock and taught me one of the most important lessons of my life in conjunction with one of my biggest sources of anxiety.

It was around fifth grade, and I was sitting at the breakfast table silently begging God to spontaneously combust all the bones in my legs as I ate my Froot Loops, and my mom could see it all over my face. Rather than coaxing me and telling me to do my best, she looked at me and, in her no-nonsense tone, asked me, "How do you think Sally Smith feels this morning?" Sally Smith was a nice girl from my class, she was an amazing artist, and she happened to be significantly overweight.

I sat there staring at my soggy cereal, trying to avoid the overwhelming Irish Catholic guilt she was laying on me, and when I said nothing, she continued. "Running the mile doesn't *actually* matter. How fast you can run around that track means nothing. But what if you found a way to be the *nicest* person on the track today? What if you did something during the mile that made someone else feel good? What if you *chose to be last*, so that someone else could tell their mom that *they* weren't?" Was my mom telling me to take my greatest fear and make it happen *on purpose*?

That day, as my class made the death march up to that track that was overgrown with weeds in a way that only Catholic school kids will understand, I found my way to the back of the line and met up with Sally.

"I hate this day," I said to her.

"Me too," she replied with a sigh.

"I'm always so nervous that I'm going to be the last one running while everyone else watches me because they've already finished the mile," I admitted.

"Me too," she replied again.

Could my mom have been right about this?

I kicked the gravel as we walked a few steps in silence, and then I blurted out, "Hey, would you want to be last together?"

She looked over at me like I was crazy, but after a second, she smiled and agreed to my weird-ass offer without any questions.

I think we jogged for two seconds of that mile simply to get out of everyone's way and spent the rest of it "power walking," laughing, and cheering on our classmates as they whizzed past us. I'm pretty sure that's the first time I said the word "bitch" out loud, in reference to my PE teacher, whom I deeply considered to be a spawn of Satan. A defining day all around. When some of my other friends saw us, they felt like they could slow down for a minute, too. I'm sure my PE teacher was pissed, but I didn't pay her much mind. I was high on the power I had over my own anxiety, and I was using it to propel myself into doing something good.

What I do remember from that day is walking off the track feeling like I had won, even though I finished dead last as the rest of the class was sitting on the sidelines catching their breath (so yes, I guess I technically "won" the losing game against Sally #oldhabitsdiehard). I was eleven years old when I learned that success doesn't have to be defined by someone else's version of "first place." It can be achieved with a little vulnerability—the ability to look outside yourself and connect with someone in a way that makes them say, "Me too."

Fast-forward many years, and while I still very much embodied "The Mile" mentality, I was setting and chasing goals based on what I *thought* I wanted. Thinking back to college and soon after graduation, I had aspirations of wanting to climb the corporate ladder in a pencil skirt, earn myself a corner office with a big window, and sit in boardrooms making decisions that made the big bucks. That's what I thought success was, because it was what had been modeled to me in the form of uncles, books I'd read, and TV shows I'd watched. In reality, when I look back at countless journals from grade school, middle school, and high school, there are pages filled with me dreaming about being a writer.

At thirteen years old I scribbled, "Have you ever wanted something so bad that you can taste it? That's how I feel about being a writer. It's this feeling I get, it's hard to explain. I get this itch, and the itch doesn't go away just by scratching it. It's below my skin, in my blood maybe. Sometimes it'll come when I'm watching TV or talking to somebody. Maybe it'll come when I'm in school. The worst is when I'm trying to sleep, but all these ideas flow through my brain: words, sentences, paragraphs, dialogues, and they're all so clear to me . . . but they don't go away until I write them down. When I'm writing, I feel like I'm with God. Maybe one day I'll be a famous writer or reporter. Maybe I'll be like Oprah. Yeah, that's how it'll be; I know it; the world doesn't just yet . . . but they better get ready."

> Success doesn't have to be defined by someone else's version of "first place." It can be achieved with a little vulnerability.

When I learned about the concept of mimetic desire from Luke Burgis's book, *Wanting*, I began to rethink what I wanted. In a nutshell, a brilliant dude named René Girard came up with this theory of mimetic desire, and he explained that once our basic needs like food, water, and shelter are met, we move into another dimension of desire where we don't have a biological "radar" or instincts to guide us. Instead, we use *other people* as a guide. If you were truly starving, you wouldn't need anyone or anything outside of yourself to signal to you that food is what you want. But when food isn't something you worry about, who do you look to to tell you what *kinds* of food to eat, what brands to buy, and what ingredients to avoid? Someone *else* who has an *outcome* that *you* desire.

Thanks to social media, our ability to identify our true desires is *fucked*. I mean, I'm a thirty-five-year-old woman who has birthed three humans, but due to the algorithm I'm sucked into on Instagram and Tik-Tok, I buy clothes based on what I see twenty-year-olds with flat stomachs and perky boobs wearing. Never mind the fact that after nursing three babies for a combined five years, my breasts better resemble tennis balls in tube socks rather than that influencer in a tube top, but nevertheless, I add that shit to my cart and am *repeatedly* humbled beyond repair when I try it on in the privacy of my own home.

Business goals are no different. We're inundated with *boss babe* narratives and six-figure business aspirations, so naturally, we adopt them as our own. *Of course* you want to have a large social media following (even though you don't bother to figure out how to engage with the smaller audience you have now). *Of course* you want to have your first $100,000 month (even though that's a completely arbitrary number). *Of course* you want to travel the world in your private jet (even though you're really a homebody). *Of course* you want to have a top-rated podcast, a twelve-step morning routine that includes guzzling celery juice even though it makes you gag, and a daily meditation practice that guides you towards flow and abundance. Because that's what *they* have. But have you ever really stopped to question what *you* actually want?

Take it from me, the recovering achievement addict (who still relapses from time to time): When your goals are deeply based in mimetic desire, you'll feel shockingly empty when you accomplish them. I was terribly confused by this for so long, and maybe you can relate? I would run so hard towards goals and accolades, and as soon as I accomplished them, I would all but shrug my shoulders and think, *Okay, what's next?* I didn't *feel* anything. There was nothing to savor because it was someone else's treat. Shit, I do this on dates with my own husband. We'll go out to eat, and no matter *what* he orders, it's automatically better than mine, and I pick off his plate until he's annoyed enough to heavily breathe, "You should have just ordered it yourself!" And then, of course, a petty argument starts and ends before we can get home and enter the next petty fight of Date Night: what to watch on TV. But the next time we go to said restaurant, I'll order what he had the last time we were there—the dish that I ignored my own plate for—and when it's delivered and placed in front of me, it's just kind of *blah*. I wanted it because that's what he wanted; I didn't want it because that's what I truly desired. There is nothing wrong with using other people's successes and desires as a guidepost for your own, but I encourage you to do a real gut check on *why* you want to summit whatever mountain it is you've set your mind to climb. While I have no doubts that you can achieve it, I'd hate for you to be disappointed by the view when you get there.

HERE'S THE PART WHERE YOU ACTUALLY DO SOMETHING

When I was thirteen years old, I knew what success felt like to me, and I bet you did, too. Take a few minutes as you sit here now and try to tap back into who you were before the world got to you. Who were you before class rankings, Instagram likes, and social media followers?

Close your eyes and take a trip up into that mind of yours. Who you were then is still in there somewhere, and maybe she's been pushed back into a far corner, but I promise that you can reach her. Do your best to call her forward, out of the dark corner, and meet her as who you are now.

- Ask her, *What is it that we wanted to be?*

- Ask her, *Who is it that we wanted to be?*

- Ask her, *What is it that we wanted to accomplish?*

If you sit with her long enough, she'll tell you, and I'm willing to bet that a portion (if not all) of it will resonate with you. Sure, maybe when you were ten years old, you wanted to be a teacher, and now at thirty-seven, you realize that's not the profession you desire, but impacting people by *teaching* may absolutely still ring true. You let the "how" of teaching (i.e., being in a traditional classroom) get in the way of the result (i.e., teaching via social media).

Next, grab your journal or computer and take some time to tap into your true desires when it comes to your business, your life, and your version of success. Let these questions, and the younger version of yourself, be the guides.

JOURNAL PROMPT FOR YOUR YOUNGER SELF:

Write a letter to your childhood self—update them on your life (the great and the not-so-great) and consider what the younger version of yourself might be proud of, surprised by, or disappointed in learning about your life. If you happen to have a photo of yourself as a child, it could be helpful to use it as a guide to help you truly picture who you're talking to. From there, imagine what the younger version of you might say in response. Write it out or meditate on it.

Journal prompt for identifying your true desires:

What lights me up is . . .

This has to have no rhyme or reason, and it needs no explanation—simply examination. Take time to pay attention to what comes up. What are you surprised by?

SCALING YOUR DESIRE

Despite what you see on social media and hear from seven-figure gurus, big goals aren't the only worthy ones. Now listen, I love a big, fat, juicy goal. Quantum leaps and unrealistic goals are the types of things that make me jump out of bed in the morning *because that's the type of person I'm hard-wired to be*. Hear me when I say that doesn't mean that's the type of person *you* have to try and become to have your goals matter. For the average person, an extra $200 to $400 a month would be considered *life-changing*. Those are the types of goals that aren't clickbaity or sexy, but they're the ones that matter just as much. My first million-dollar year felt the same type of exciting and important as my first $500 paycheck, and both were extremely worthy and significant. So whether you're starting an Etsy shop that sells handmade llama figurines or you're taking up photography as a side hustle, your goals don't have to be massive for you to take them seriously and plan accordingly.

While we'll get there later on in the book, this is not the section about money. If your goal is solely money-based, you've failed the assignment. While money can (and arguably should) absofreakinlutely be a driving goal, we also need a substance goal to make it sustainable.

I'm not a health or fitness fanatic, but I find they're the two topics that make fabulous metaphors for business examples. Case in point: I have a history of a shitty relationship with food, and years ago when I was working with a registered dietician to *learn* about food rather than *fear* it, I was surprised when she explained the importance of pairing certain foods together. She told me that rather than eating just a carb, it would be more advantageous if I paired the carb with a protein or a healthy fat. Doing so would stabilize my blood sugar, therefore helping me stay satiated longer. That's how I think about money goals and substance goals. I am extremely money-motivated, but I've found that when you're only working for a dollar amount, you will never feel fully satisfied. Just like eating a piece of bread isn't bad, it would keep me satisfied longer if I paired it with some nut butter. When it comes to substance goals, we can break them down into three categories: lifestyle, time, and purpose.

LIFESTYLE GOALS

Lifestyle goals are common and massively motivating. Maybe you've been desiring to improve your health, and you've been wanting to pull the trigger on joining the local Pilates studio but haven't because the cost of the monthly membership makes you sweat. Money is tied to this goal, but it has a purpose behind it, other than "make so much money so I can swim in a room of it," Scrooge McDuck style.

When I first started my entrepreneurial journey, I wanted to be able to shop at Target and add a t-shirt to my cart without having to have the internal dialogue surrounding whether it was *worth* $15.99. I wanted to live the kind of lifestyle where if I wanted that top, I'd buy it, damn it. At that time in my life, *that* was the kind of lifestyle I could wrap my head around achieving. It wasn't about living a lifestyle that included investing, making millions, or treating my family and friends to fun vacations; it was about being able to treat myself without feeling guilty. When I got to the point that I could comfortably buy not one, but *two* tops at Target whenever I wanted, I adjusted my lifestyle goals to include things like being able to afford a house cleaner once a month because it would alleviate stress by taking one thing off my to-do list and open up more time to spend with my family.

Today, my lifestyle goals include things that would have never crossed my mind as a potential possibility six years ago, but they are no less important than the lifestyle goals I started with. It's unpopular to say in the self-help world, but your goals don't need to be quantum leaps to justify being excited about them. You can bet your sweet ass that when I got to the place where I was making enough money to buy a few tops at Target without having to consider moving money from my savings account, I celebrated that shit. I want you to cultivate a sense of excitement around where you're headed on the first stop of your journey, and I want you to squash the idea that you need to be at a certain level of flashiness before you can start talking about and celebrating your wins. If you bought the shirt and it felt easier than it has in the past, it's perfectly acceptable to share that sense of accomplishment with your social media audience, to take them on a journey where you tell them, "You know what? Five months ago, I wouldn't have bought this shirt *just because*, because, well . . . things felt a little tight in the purse string department. I overthought every single purchase I made for myself because it felt like I could buy this shirt for me *or* buy one for my kid. Today, I'm in a space where it's an *and*, and well . . . that feels good, damn it."

So many people I work with are blinded by what I call the "Six-Figure Fairytale"—this idea that life and goals and accomplishments only become golden once they've entered the Land of the Six-Figure Business. You're given some glass slippers and—poof!—you're in a ballgown clinking champagne flutes with rich people and are handed a permission slip that permits you to start celebrating. I say fuck that. A glass slipper sounds terribly uncomfortable, and honestly, I'd be too concerned about it shattering and slicing my foot in half to enjoy anything about champagne flutes and golden dreams. Give me my sneakers and my Target cart and let me be on my merry way.

Now, what if you're someone who's already clinking champagne flutes in the Six-Figure Fairytale, and the idea of shopping at Target bores you? Fantastic. Wonderful. And also, so what? You, too, have to attach a goal outside of *just* money to keep climbing that golden ladder to the Land of the Seven-Figure Fairytale and beyond.

As my business and brand grew, it was easy to slip into a money-only goal-setting territory, so it's a constant effort to recalibrate. Any time I find myself focusing on and attaching myself to monetary goals and outcomes, I do something kind for someone else. Maybe it's sending a Starbucks gift card to a friend or making cookies for my kids' classes; it doesn't matter, it simply needs to be something that pulls me outside of the money-hungry vortex and into my life that I'm extremely grateful to be living.

TIME GOALS

I grew up in an incredibly blue-collar family; my mom was a flight attendant, and my dad worked in retail sales. Neither of them went to college, and I was aware of the money we *didn't* have from a young age. We didn't have some of the material things that my cousins or peers had, *but* I had an abundance of time with my family in a way that many of my friends *didn't* have with their parents. My parents were always there to pick us up after school, we had dinner together every single night, and my parents never missed a sporting or school event for my brother and me. Growing up, there were absolutely times when I felt a desire for things we couldn't afford, but now as an adult, I'm acutely aware that money is an infinite resource, and time is not.

As cliché as it sounds (trust me, I'm half gagging as I type this), I didn't fully realize this until I had my own kids. Before I had kids, I didn't care if I needed to work long hours, travel during the week, or attend networking happy hours. After I had my first baby, all of that came to a screeching halt. I didn't want to have to send Jack to daycare and have someone else tell me about the milestones he was reaching. I wanted to be the one to take him to story time at the library, make him lunch, and kiss his boo-boos. I deeply desired to be as present as possible.

Again, this is a goal that is directly related to money, but there's a reason behind it. Having a goal of "I want my business to make $75,000 a year" is vastly different from "I need my business to make $75,000 a year so I can stay home with my kids." If you don't have the substance tied to it, you don't experience the satisfaction when you achieve it, and then you're left feeling empty and in search of your next goal to hit.

PURPOSE-DRIVEN GOALS

When I started my Instagram account, @noshamesalesgame, my goal was to change the perception of network marketing from the inside out. Network marketing was something that changed the trajectory of my life, but it was able to do so because I did it my way (and without some antiquated "hey girl" cold messaging approach). I wanted to help modernize an industry that so desperately needs it.

I had a client, Ashley, who wanted to build a successful side business not so she could stay home with her children, but so she could increase her charitable giving. She had two foundations that were extremely important to her, and she wanted to make more money so it could go towards these causes she was passionate about.

Ashley's best friend, Kendra, was diagnosed with breast cancer, and she started a GoFundMe page so that Kendra and her family wouldn't have to worry about medical bills. She decided to become a consultant with a network marketing company solely to donate her paycheck every month to Kendra's foundation (to which she was able to donate thousands). You don't have to want to change an industry or give all your profits away to charity; it's simply about attaching yourself to something that's *bigger* than you.

HERE'S THE PART WHERE YOU ACTUALLY DO SOMETHING

Let's come up with your definition of success.

For example, part of my personal definition of success is being able to do what I want, when I want, with who I want.

Start by setting a timer for five minutes and doing a brain dump of anything and everything that you would define as success. Please do me a solid and don't think too hard here; there's no need to be realistic or "safe." Just let it flow.

Brain Dump of Success list

_____

_____

_____

_____

_____

_____

_____

_____

_____

_____

_____

After you have your Brain Dump of Success list, I want you to see if you can identify any themes.

When I did this years ago, I had things on my list like a weekly house cleaner, monthly facials, an updated wardrobe. To me, it became clear that I wanted to be able to invest in myself in ways that weren't feasible at that time (a.k.a.: to do what *I* want).

I also noticed that I had things on my list like traveling with my husband and attending certain events like concerts and personal development retreats with my friends, and those things would require a massive level of time freedom and flexibility (a.k.a.: to do what I want, *when* I want). Lastly, I noticed that the bulk of my list was dedicated to being able to give to my family, friends, and charities in ways that didn't seem even remotely possible at that time. I wanted to buy my mom a house, I wanted to treat my best friend to a tropical vacation, I wanted to give my children experiences, and I wanted to live life with my husband by my side as much as possible (a.k.a.: to do what I want, when I want, with *who* I want).

For this process, you'll have to intentionally turn down the noise of the outside world and tune inwards. It can feel awkward and uncomfortable at first, like going out to lunch with a friend you haven't seen or talked to in a long while, but ultimately, you're able to pick up right where you left off.

Lastly, when you have nailed down your definition of success, I need you to write it down. I'm partial to pen and paper (hashtag team old-school), but if making an image and saving it as the background on your phone is more your speed, go for it. The idea is that I want it to be outside of your head in a way that you can see it, learn it, and believe it to be true.

*Note: *I'm absolutely aware that the desires I expressed in this chapter are drenched in privilege. I understand that for many people, not sending their kids to daycare isn't an option. I also understand that not everyone desires—or is able—to have children. Whatever your goal is, it is valid.*

Chapter 04

FACING
THE F-WORD

So now that we know where you're headed, and you've got the car filled with gas and your favorite snacks next to you in the front seat, we have to prepare for the inevitable roadblocks and detours you'll encounter along the way.

You might be thinking, *Damn it, Colleen, why are you being such a Negative Nancy? I'm a positive thinker and am manifesting millions, so I refuse to focus on anything that's not love and light.*

To that I say, "That's cute, Jan."

Co-creating epic shit with the Universe (or God or Allah or whatever you want to call it) is my favorite thing to do; but putting your head in the sand like a confused dodo bird, expecting that you won't have any mental gremlins attempt to derail your ride, is a sick joke to play on yourself. The truth is, the sooner you can identify all the fears and bullshit stories that will do their damnedest to sabotage you, the sooner you'll be equipped to knock those sonsabitches *out*, and keep freaking going.

FEAR OF SUCCESS

It sounds crazy, right? I mean, we're all here to achieve our version of success; it's literally what we want, so how in the hell could that be scary? Never in a million years would I have even *considered* that success, the thing I was chasing most, would be the thing that scared me. It wasn't until I read the book *The Big Leap* by Gay Hendricks that I had my "holy shit" moment of clarity. In the book (that you absolutely must read, by the way), Hendricks explains the Upper Limit Problem, a concept that we each have an "inner thermostat" setting that regulates how much awesomeness we allow ourselves to enjoy at any given time. Be it love, money, friendships, or the flow of creativity, we each have an internal setting of what we're used to and what feels good and safe. When we do something, like make a shit-ton more money than we're used to, it triggers our thermostat setting to rise, and we'll subconsciously do something to sabotage ourselves, to lower the thermostat back down to a place where we feel more comfortable and secure. There have been so many times in my career that the Upper Limit Problem was on full display, and I had no idea.

When I started my coaching and consulting business, I was bound and determined to grow it into a massive agency where I would work with corporations to provide professional development to their leadership teams. I made the website, got professional photos taken, ordered business cards, and created my offerings. I was set to jet, my friends. You can imagine how elated I was when I signed my first contract with a local company for fifteen hundred dollars. (I could also write a book on what it's like to undercharge for your services, but we'll save that for another time.) Fifteen hundred dollars was a *big deal* to me, and I was on cloud nine . . . until I wasn't.

I found myself quickly irritated with my contact at the company. I got migraines before two separate meetings. I was consumed with worry that certain people at the company thought I was incompetent (even though they had given me *no actual reason* to think that). By the time our contract was up, I was miserable and ended up ghosting my contact. She followed up several times, asking if they could schedule certain trainings and workshops, and I just didn't answer. It's horribly embarrassing to admit, but it's the truth.

Let's not forget the time Cory and I made an offer on an investment property. We had been looking into buying our first investment property for several months because we were ready to add another stream of revenue to the mix. We had done the research, run the numbers, and told our realtor what we were looking for. It all made sense, and we were excited about this new adventure into the world of rental properties. After months of searching, a perfect house hit the market. We drove two hours out to a mountain resort and fell in love with a newly renovated cabin. It was everything we wanted. Not only could I envision it easily being a successful vacation rental, but I could also envision weekend trips that we could make as a family—skiing, snow tubing, swimming, and creating so many wonderful memories with our boys. On the drive home, we were buzzing with nervous excitement. We talked about how we'd manage it as a rental property and how I could use social media to market it, and when we got home to run the numbers, we decided to make an offer on the house. It was accepted the next day, and we were ecstatic. I sent the listing to several of my closest friends and family, feeling over-the-top excitement and pride that I was in a place in my life where I could afford to do something like buy an investment property. I was on cloud nine . . . until I wasn't.

I quickly found myself anxious about the down payment. Although we could have easily swung it, I was fearful that all future money would stop flowing. I voiced my concern about managing a property that was two hours away; what if something happened and we had to drive out there? Could I even trust a rental management company? The more I thought about it, the more I convinced myself that we (I) didn't have the bandwidth to take this on. Cory gave me very logical solutions to all of my concerns, and yet I couldn't bring myself to go through with it. We called the realtor the next night and withdrew our offer.

I could give you a dozen more examples of how I've let my fear of success sabotage a good thing, but I think you get the picture (and maybe you can relate). Here's the thing: My fear of success hasn't gone away; I've simply learned to manage it. I name it to tame it, and I take bold actions.

When I created my membership site, Direct Sales Growth Community, our goal was to have it be a nice supplemental income to help with our dismal financial situation. After running the numbers, Cory and I forecasted it bringing in somewhere in the ballpark of $30,000 a *year*, and we were *stoked* by the idea of it all. It had been four years and we were still living in the tiny old house that we moved into after we had to sell our dream home, and it still felt like a massive fuck you from the Universe. We had acquired a suffocating amount of debt, and I was pissed about it; it felt like no matter what happened, we couldn't get ahead.

There were many nights when Cory and I sat in our front dining-room-turned-office and cried, or fought, or cried and fought. We didn't know how we were going to pay the bills, we had kids to feed and clothe, and we questioned our sanity more times than I can count. There was a stretch of time when Cory was job searching because we didn't know how much longer we could try to make our businesses work. He went on several interviews, but every time an offer came in, there'd be a wink from the Universe in the form of a new client or a glowing testimonial from an existing one. While we were absolutely drowning financially, we still had this glimmer of hope that we could make it work. We knew if anyone could do it, it was us, and while it made us overwhelmingly anxious, we always chose to stay the course over choosing comfort.

Based on that depressing situation, you can imagine how I felt when, not long after launching DSGC, we had our first $30,000 *month*. As I type this and am brought back to that day (less than three years ago, I might add), I buzz with excitement for that version of myself. She danced in her kitchen, cry-laughing at her good fortune, thinking she had hit the jackpot, that it couldn't get better than that moment. But she had no idea what greatness was right around the corner.

I think back to when I started making more money than I could have ever imagined; it felt so exciting and impossible at the same time. There were many times that I thought, *Well, this is a fluke; it can't possibly happen again next month*, but because I was aware of my Upper Limit Problem, I would ask myself, *But why can't it happen again next month?* And when I had no good answers other than fear-based ones, I was able to sit with both the overwhelming excitement and gratitude, as well as the overwhelming discomfort of smashing my "internal thermostat" off the wall. So now, when six-figure *months* have become normal, rather than allowing myself to run to my internal thermostat and try and find a comfortable temperature, I sit with any discomfort and anxiety and know it will pass.

Whatever your definition of success is, I'm willing to bet you've been closer to it than you even realize, but you're equating the heat with fear. It makes me think of that silly "hot or cold" game I play with my kids, where I'll hide something and they walk around with no clues other than me saying "colder" as they move away from it and "hotter" as they move closer. If heat means you're close, and when it feels like the Universe is screaming "Hot! Hot! Hot!" it doesn't mean you're off track; it means you're exactly in the place you've been trying to find.

FEAR OF BEING SALESY

For the longest time, when I thought of sales, I immediately pictured Danny DeVito's character in *Matilda*: a fast-talking, dishonest, no-good used car *salesman*. (No shade to used car salesmen, by the way. My dad sold cars for many years!) He (DeVito) walked around in cheap suits, fake gold chains, and slicked-back hair, doing and saying whatever he needed to make a sale. Whether or not you picture this very specific character in your mind, if you're scared of sales, you know what I'm talking about. In your mind, sales equals gross. I'd challenge that thought process, though, because selling isn't the root issue; it's money (which is what we cover in the next section!).

Back to Matilda's dad for a sec. He was gross and slimy because it was obvious that the sale came before and above the customer. He didn't care if the car he was selling was a lemon; he cared about the money. You're different, though, because you *do* care about the clients and customers you're serving. That, and you believe in the products and services that you provide. When people think of being "salesy," they're typically concerned about bothering other people, or seeming desperate to make a transaction. That's all some perception bullshit that we need to clean up. Mmkay, Pumpkin?

When you check your email today, I'm certain you'll have at least one message in your inbox from a company trying to sell you something. Whether it's Nordstrom telling you about the newest line of spring dresses, Bath & Body Works alerting you that their three-wick candles are buy one, get one free, or Uber Eats sending you a coupon, it's *all* sales. Whether or not you open them and take advantage of the offer, you're not thinking, *God, I wish Nordstrom would just stop being so damn salesy all the time. They never even ask how I'm doing.* Of course not! If Nordstrom sent me an email telling me they think my kids are so cute and they loved the last Reel I posted, and oh, by the way, check out these spring dresses, it would be ridiculous (and flagged as spam). I expect Nordstrom to sell to me because they're a legitimate business. If you come across as salesy, it's not the selling that gives people the ick— it's your approach.

Now, obviously, Nordstrom is a billion-dollar conglomerate, and you might not be, but the same principles can be applied. You can show up as a professional, add value, and sell to people every damn day without ever feeling (or looking) salesy, but you have to believe it.

FEAR OF PEOPLE JUDGING YOU

I recently polled my Instagram audience of 143,000 people and asked if fear of internet trolls leaving a mean comment or sending a nasty DM kept them from showing up as their quirky, potentially unshowered, f-bomb-dropping selves on social media. My bet was on a resounding yes, but I couldn't have been more wrong. I got so many DMs that it took me two days to read and respond to them, and the answer was overwhelmingly the same: "I'm not worried about faceless people on the internet; I'm worried about the people in my social circles judging me."

Maybe it's because I'm used to faceless people on the internet judging me, or maybe it's because the people in my inner circle aren't jackasses, but I hear you. I don't quite get you, but I hear you. My friend Shauna VanBogart (who you absolutely must follow on Instagram, by the way, @shaunavanbogart) made a comment recently that blew my mind wide open and helped me see the mass of people who are fearful of their inner social circles seeing (and judging) them through a different lens. This is a weird-ass time to be an entrepreneur, mainly because of the internet. When baby boomers went to work every day, they had the ability to be an entirely different person. I often joked with my mom that she had her "phone voice" and her real voice, because if she happened to get a call from work, her voice raised three octaves and she sounded nothing like herself. But that's how they knew her, right? It didn't make their heads tilt in bewilderment because that was the only voice they'd heard. In today's world, for those of us who are building brands and businesses, we have to do it in front of everyone. Not only are you attending the new age board meeting on IG Live, where your potential clients and target audience can tune in, but so can your Aunt Sheryl, who knows nothing about whatever it is that you're selling (but she'll absolutely be the first one to give you feedback).

While my mom is immensely proud of me, she has no idea what the hell it is that I do. Case in point: I have built a seven-figure online membership community in two years, and she refers to it as my "club." And even though she's been telling me my *entire life* that I should write a book, when I told her that I was finally writing this one, she said, "But will you have enough time to still make money with your club?" I *passionately* explained that writing a book was going to help further my "club" along and help me build my brand even more. I told her it would help me be seen as an expert (she giggled) and that it made perfect business sense, and then I moved on. It was also a reminder that for many entrepreneurs, the people you're closest to won't understand what it is that you do, and while the natural reaction is to try to explain yourself until you're blue in the face, it's not mission critical for them to "get" it. If I was so concerned about my mom understanding what it is that I do, I wouldn't be in the game. But you know what? Even though I know I'm the more skilled entrepreneur between the two of us, I still hear her questions on the days when I'm sitting here and seemingly can't string a sentence together without wanting to throw my computer into a fiery dumpster. Mastering the skill of discernment is one of the most powerful things I've done for my business. I absolutely hear her well-meaning-but-no-idea-what-she's-talking-about questions in my difficult moments, but I don't let them in the driver's seat of my metaphorical car. I strap them in the backseat, turn up my 2000s pop hits playlist, and choose to move forward. I'm fortunate enough to have a parent who supports me and loves me, and I'm also okay with the fact that she has no clue who I am in my professional life. I have nothing to prove. I also know that's not a universal experience.

If your reality falls along the line of "unsupportive family and friends," it also doesn't help that social media makes every day Bring Your Mom (or judgy neighbor/aunt/friend from high school) to Work Day. It feels like you have her (or your friends or your acquaintances) standing right behind you at work, questioning everything you do—and that can feel mighty distracting, stifling, and just plain uncomfortable.

Here's the truth of the matter: The people in your life who judge you are the ones who can see you're changing, and it holds up a mirror to the fact that they're not. No one who is growing and developing as a human will ever look at someone else doing the same thing and talk down to them. Ever. The people who judge are the ones who feel insecure about the fact that their lives are staying the same. For some people, staying the same is what they *want* to do, so they don't judge you! For others, they wish they could change, but they make the choice to stay the same, so they judge you instead.

This isn't me just blowing sunshine up your ass; it's an actual cultural phenomenon, most commonly known as Tall Poppy Syndrome. It's the idea that rather than celebrating your achievements, others instead put a target on your back, attempting to knock you down a peg or two. In Japan, there is a similar expression: "The tallest nail gets hammered down." It's also been described as the "crab bucket mentality"—because when you're cooking crabs in a pot or bucket, a lid isn't needed. If one crab gets too close to the top, the other crabs in the pot will pull it back down.

Basically, for a massive number of people, it feels really shitty when they see someone else succeeding when they're not. When you're criticized for your success, it carries the implication that maybe you don't actually deserve it, which is an absolute mindfuck that no one deserves.

Call it Tall Poppy Syndrome, or jealousy, or mean people just plain sucking, but judging people isn't always that big of a deal. People are judging you all the time. The other thing? *You* are judging everyone else all the time, too. So let me subtly hold up a hand and invite you down off your high horse so we can have a rational conversation about it. That's right, take my hand; you're doing it. . . . Ah, yes, here we are on solid ground. Welcome back to reality.

> Here's the truth of the matter: The people in your life who judge you are the ones who can see you're changing, and it holds up a mirror to the fact that they're not.

On the most basic human level, making judgments is how we survive in this world. We make judgments about who is safe, who benefits us, and how to simply not get ourselves killed on any given day. But also, I know you judge the shit out of people for pettier reasons. Maybe the woman in front of you in line at Starbucks is wearing a perfume that makes you gag. *Judging.* Maybe your coworker brings in tuna fish for the third day in a row, and you think she's rude. *Judging.* Maybe you see someone on social media post about their engagement, and the first thing you do is zoom in on the ring. *Judy McJudgerson.*

And what *actually* happens as a result in any of those scenarios? Not a damn thing. I'm assuming you don't tap the woman in front of you and tell her she smells like your grandmother's favorite potpourri. I'm willing to bet you don't say anything to Tuna Tessie, and I'm going to go out on a limb and guess that you don't leave a comment on the engagement post with your two cents that he could have done better.

Of course not. What's utterly fantastic about all of this is that those people get to go on with their lives in blissful peace—smelling, eating, and celebrating the way that their little hearts' desire.

The same goes for you, my scaredy cat friend. EVEN IF someone thinks you're weird for selling your product or service, talking about your business, or showing up confidently online . . . *so what?*

So. Fucking. What?

We're not in middle school anymore, Brittany. We don't need everyone to like us, and we're sure as hell not going to try and be for everyone. Why? Repeat after me, my friends: "If you try to be for everyone, you'll end up being for no one."

Your mom, aunt, second cousin twice removed, or that chick from high school are not going to make or break your business. Remember this: You're here to focus on your bottom line, not how you're perceived in someone else's mind.

It can also be people you *don't* know, though. For me, I get judged on the internet every single day. Shit, I was doing a training on Instagram Live just yesterday, and there was a jackass in the Live comments section saying things like "Could you be any uglier?" and "You probably don't have a real husband because no man could be attracted to a butch woman like you." (I tell you what, no one gets more triggered by a woman with short hair than a man with a small dick.) Whenever I make content about network marketing being a smart choice for many people, I get comments about how wrong I am, how much of a scammer I am, and how I couldn't be any worse of a person. The amazing thing is that the rational side of my brain knows those things aren't true, but there's also a part of me that wants to turn down my volume or not show up as much because of the fear of someone judging me or being mean. I see this reaction in other online entrepreneurs all the time, too. Whether you have 140,000 or 140 followers, a mean comment is a mean comment, and it stings. I've found that to avoid that unpleasant feeling, many entrepreneurs start to make content based on what they think the judgy people will say, rather than creating content for the people who need their unique message. My advice to you (and myself) is to get crystal freaking clear on *who* you're talking to and showing up for—and not be distracted by the people you fear.

FEAR OF BEING SEEN

Like I mentioned, when I started the @noshamesalesgame Instagram account, I had no intention of ever associating it with *me*, so it was completely anonymous. I was a nothing, nobody, known by absolutely no one, but I preferred that. The account wasn't supposed to be about me; it was supposed to be about the industry and helping change the perception of it from the inside out. But when people in my real life started to catch on and call me out, I panicked. My cover had been blown, and I needed to introduce myself before someone else did it for me. I cannot tell you how absolutely terrifying that decision was for me. I was so proud of—and excited by—the momentum the account was gaining, but I was sure if people saw that it was me (again, a nobody), it would be dead in the water. I congratulated myself on a wave well ridden, and all but packed up my virtual boxes the day before hopping on video for the first time. "It was fun while it lasted," I told Cory, certain as all get-out that we had reached the end of the road. But then a crazy thing happened: People didn't hate the fact that it was me, and the account didn't die. I was so perplexed when the account *kept growing*, convinced that people sharing my content just hadn't *seen me* yet. I was bracing myself for the virtual tomatoes to be thrown right in my face, but they never came. I think that's a feeling that so many of my fellow entrepreneurs can probably relate to. You start this thing without many expectations, but if you give it actual effort, people are going to have to *see you*. And that shit is terrifying. But I'm here to remind you that you can only get so far without being fully seen. I know it's scary to put yourself out there, to have people see you *try*, and to risk not being liked or accepted by everyone. But even when it feels like the walls will crumble if you're actually *seen*, the reality is that the foundation is settling into place.

FEAR OF MONEY

If we're going to talk about sales, we're going to have to talk about money. Over the last few years, I've made a lot of it, I've helped other people do the same, and the thing I've learned is that we have some *fucked-up shit* swirling around in our heads about money.

Did you know that anxiety and excitement are caused by the same chemical reaction in your brain, but how you interpret the physical symptoms determines how you perceive what's going on in that noggin of yours?

As someone with a diagnosed anxiety disorder, this blows my mind. But I also know that it tracks. For God's sake, I can't even do cardio exercises because if my heart rate increases above a certain rate, I think I'm having a heart attack. Even when I am *completely aware* that I'm running, if I feel my heart beat faster than it normally does, my brain bypasses any ounce of logic and goes straight to catastrophe.

That's kind of like selling and recommending. It's the same thing, but how we react to it determines our perception. Do you think it's gross and it makes you uncomfortable, or do you know it's something we all do every day of our lives, and it excites you?

I'm willing to bet that you have no problem whatsoever hopping on social media or texting your best friend about the new true crime documentary you just watched.

I'm confident that you'd have no issue sharing with anyone who would listen that the dress you bought was not only on sale, but it *HAS POCKETS.*

I'm also sure that you wouldn't think twice before sharing the link to the sunglasses you just bought.

You do understand that all of that is selling, don't you?

You just don't get paid for it.

But it's as if some little confidence-killing ninjas seep into your skull and make you believe that if you're selling something that actually makes you money . . . it's bad.

So here's where I need you to get really real with yourself. Are you scared to sell, or are you scared for people to know that you're making (or trying to make) money?

I don't want you to feel embarrassed or trip into some shame spiral if you realize that you're concerned that making money comes with some judgment from others. Women have been generationally fucked when it comes to our money mindsets. I mean, honestly, can you imagine a dude worrying about making money? Fretting over the fact that his network might know that he's out there building a brand? Distraught that someone might think he's "bad" for being rich?

Those are laughable scenarios. But swap the genitalia of the main character in these examples, and it tracks.

For the longest time, I believed that wanting money made me greedy and gross. And I don't know about you, but being greedy and gross isn't a look I'm after. It's almost as if I wore my "I don't want money" badge with pride. *I* didn't need dirty, greedy money. *I* was nice and kind and helped others. *I* didn't need money to do or be any of that. And because I had this deep-seated aversion to making money, my actions helped me confirm that (lack of) desire. I worked, sure. But I didn't expect more, let alone ever imagine asking for more.

When it came down to it, I had a firm belief that I had to choose between being *good* and being *rich*. And like many women I know and work with, being good and nice and liked is almost more important than oxygen.

I can honestly picture badge-wearing, anti-money me sitting in a room with someone as the space was drained of oxygen, and I'd be like

Me? No, no . . . I can't quite breathe in here, but it's fine. Are you mad at me?

It wasn't until I made the connection that money is energy that things changed for me and how I showed up to sell. Instead of thinking, *Oh, I'm taking money from them if they buy my Unicorn Tears*, I now view it as a completely even energy exchange. They're exchanging their energy (money) with my energy (my service offering). It's a perfectly balanced energy transaction.

Having more energy can only be a positive thing, too. When I have more energy, I can do more *good* in this world. For example, designated gift-giving days like Christmas or birthdays completely stunt my creativity, but a random "just because" act of kindness brings me immense joy. When I was broke, I couldn't do the things I get to do now but so desperately desired then.

When I was an energetic money repellant, I couldn't do things like leave a $100 tip for the pregnant waitress at the breakfast diner we stopped by while on a road trip. I couldn't send my friend wine and her favorite chocolate when she had a miscarriage, and I lived six hours away. I couldn't buy my mom a house, like I had always dreamt of doing. Why? Because I was waving a big ol' energetic middle finger to the Universe's ability to have money flow my way.

I'll never forget walking into Target one afternoon at the tail end of the summer. They were partnered with a local school district and were running a program to help fill backpacks for children in need as we headed into the school year. My heart leapt with joy—this was my jam. I grabbed the school supply list for a first grader and made my way to the happiest aisle of all: the fully stocked school supply section. I found an adorable backpack covered in blue sharks; it was *$16.99.*

And so, I started the mental calculation of everything I was adding to my cart.

Folders, pencils, markers, crayons, glue sticks, mini white boards, notebooks, a ruler; all in all, it would have cost me somewhere in the ballpark of $50. I stood in the school supply section—normally a spot that evoked pure happiness and excitement in me—and felt hot tears hitting my eyes. I knew I had about $120 in my account, and I needed to make it through another week. There was no way I was going to be able to swing this. I hate to admit it, but I left the cart right in the middle of the aisle, bolted to my car, and cried.

I cried because I finally realized that having money wasn't about yachts and Hummers with gold rims and wearing those Gucci velour tracksuits that make people's faces look extremely punchable. It was about having good intentions, helping others, and being able to match my behaviors with those desires.

I don't know how long I sat there feeling sorry for myself, and for the kid who I was trying to help, but I know filling a backpack for a kid in need became an overwhelming motivation for me. Something shifted within me, and I knew that my approach to sales and making money was forever changed.

HERE'S THE PART WHERE YOU ACTUALLY DO SOMETHING

What is that money-making motivator for you?

What would you do for yourself and others if you had all the money you desired? Take some time to journal about who you'd impact and how, and how it would make you *feel*.

For me, it wasn't the actual filling of the backpack that fueled me. That situation served as an important catalyst, but it was far bigger than that one moment. I knew that if I wanted to impact others, I'd have to clean up the way I felt about sales and making money.

Chapter 05

HERE'S WHERE I CALL YOU ON YOUR BULLSHIT

T his is where I'm usually met with a deer-in-the-headlights look, because the majority of people have convinced themselves that their excuses are their realities. After working with thousands of women in the entrepreneurial space, I've identified the most common bullshit stories that we tell ourselves, and I'm going to walk you through each of them (and then, of course, we're going to work through your personal bullshit stories because that's where the magic happens. Buckle up, buttercup, here we go.) Let's start with the one I hear the most, shall we?

BULLSHIT STORY #1: *I'm afraid people won't like me*

As a person with somewhat of a social media presence, I learned quickly that no matter what you say or how you say it, you're bound to piss someone off. I've been sent a meme on several occasions that reads something like:

How Social Media Works

Me: "I prefer dogs to cats."

Random Person on the Internet: "So basically, what you're saying is that you hate cats. You also failed to mention ferrets, goldfish, hamsters, and birds. Educate yourself, you toxic piece of human garbage. I'm literally shaking omg."

On top of that, even if you *did* mention ferrets, goldfish, hamsters, and birds, there are going to be people who *simply do not like you.*

I recently had what I know to be many of your worst social media nightmares happen to me. Following the 2023 Super Bowl, I created a piece of content relating to Rihanna's halftime show. The image said:

Rihanna just performed the Super Bowl halftime show while pregnant. You're not too tired or busy to work on your business today.

The caption read:

I'm Rihanna neutral, but I was in awe seeing her perform that halftime show as a pregnant woman.

Like, either you're a boss bitch who gets it done, or you're not (and if that triggers you, you have your answer).

Pick your lane, and LFG.

I hit post, and then went on my merry way. About twenty minutes later, I was in the middle of a workout, and my husband texted me, "Way to trigger some people this morning." To which I responded, "That's showbiz, Baby," and kept on going without a second thought. Normally, if I have any sort of opinion or "spicy" content, the internet trolls come out from under their bridges with their virtual pitchforks and congregate in my comments section. After another fifteen minutes had passed, a good friend called me, and when I saw her name pop up, I knew it had to be about the post. I answered the phone, and she said, "Solidarity, sister! People are crazy!" At that point, I realized I might have a situation on my hands. With one eye open, I headed over to Instagram to see what the trolls had to say . . . only to be shocked that it *wasn't* the trolls. It was my audience, people who typically liked my content.

The outrage was intense in the comments section, and things were taken up a notch in my DMs.

"You're a toxic human."

"You're an absolute embarrassment to the women's movement."

"I hope you get canceled."

"I hope you die."

. . . over an Instagram post.

Maybe it's because I'm two and a half years in and I've grown a thick skin, but I was, for the most part, quite unphased. It absolutely stung, but I didn't cry, I didn't have an anxiety attack, I didn't edit my post, and I didn't apologize.

A close friend and fellow entrepreneur confided in me, saying, "I think I want to be well-known, but I know I wouldn't be able to handle what's going on over on your Instagram today." That's when I realized (or, more accurately, remembered) that people are so fearful of not being liked. Do I want everyone to like me? Sure. I'd also like a pet unicorn, but that's not going to happen either. When it comes to the noise of the naysayers, you have to consider the source before you allow it to consume you. I surround myself with trusted people whom I respect immensely and wholeheartedly. When I need help figuring out if I need to course correct or stand my ground, those are the ones I turn to for guidance. Note: these are not "yes people." They are the ones that will tell me, "Colleen, you fucked up and need to fix it," without any hesitation. When all of them said, "People missed the point, and that's not on you," I let it go and went on with my day.

When it comes to people on the internet not liking you, you have to discern between feelings and facts. Sure, when people are heated and disagreeing in my comments section and DMs, I feel a rollercoaster of emotions. That day, I *felt* shocked, confused, and disappointed. The *facts* told a different story, though. While the average number of likes on my previous five posts was 3,647, the post that made me feel *shocked, confused, and disappointed* got over 11,000 likes and over 780 comments in twenty-four hours. That post <u>alone</u> brought in seventy followers that day, all my insights were trending upward, and I did over $4,000 in sales within those same twenty-four hours.

When you're creating content that makes people feel something, it's not always going to be positive. Not everyone will like you, but the right ones will.

Those are some fears, but what about the added layer of the bullshit stories we tell ourselves? What's scary about our bullshit stories is that they can oftentimes be difficult to identify. We have them on a loop in our heads, so much so that we've heard them enough times that we actually believe them to be true. Normally, the bullshit stories sound a bit like . . .

BULLSHIT STORY #2: "I'm just a . . ."

If I could make a dime for any time I heard the "I don't have anything to talk about, I'm *just* a . . . (fill in the blank)" line, I'd have another multimillion-dollar stream of income on my hands. Newsflash: you're not boring, you're just bored. The "I'm boring" or "I'm just a . . ." is a bullshit story and one that many of us find comfort in buying into, because it's easy to believe that you're boring and have nothing of value to add. We find comfort in it because if we believe that we're boring and no one cares about anything we have to say, we don't need to show up. If we don't need to show up, we don't need to be uncomfortable! But, friends, comfort often acts like your gaslighting ex-boyfriend (who you got rid of for a reason). I'm confident that you've had some version of an excuse rattle around your brain at some point:

I'm *just* a mom.

I'm *just* a teacher.

I'm *just* a single chick with seventeen cats.

I'm *just* an underwater basket weaver.

Just, just, justifying why you think you're boring and can't connect with anyone. The reality of the matter? Now, more than ever, people are craving human connection. They want to see themselves in other people and know that they aren't alone. Dare I say, gone are the days of us average people trying to be influencers with perfectly curated lives and aesthetically pleasing feeds.

When I see a woman posting pictures in her stark white kitchen with her three children dressed in neutral-colored monogrammed smocks, eating organic kale salads straight from their backyard garden, I simply cannot relate. Because meanwhile, I'm over here on the other side of the screen in my kitchen with pretzel sticks and Goldfish crumbs all over the floor. I'm dodging neon-colored Nerf footballs that my boys (who also have unbridled, unwarranted confidence in dressing themselves) throw to each other without caution, and I'm pretty sure they survive off frozen chicken nuggets. Don't worry, I heat them up first (because I'm a *good mom*).

So listen, if that influencer's perfectly curated picture is her genuine reality, I love that journey for her. But we're not speaking the same language, and when you're not speaking the same energetic language as the people who are watching you, they won't end up buying from you.

The great news is, your "mundane" life is the content that your audience will connect with, and showing up in whatever season of life you're in is your value add. Better yet, when you show up "as is," it gives your audience the permission (a.k.a. confidence) to do the same.

I once followed a chick on Instagram who was talking about how her son always left socks around the house. No matter what room she was in, there was a random sock, shed like snakeskin, from her smelly preteen son. So, she made it a content thing, taking us through the rooms of her house, looking for lone socks. People were chiming in, making bets on how many she'd find, and laughing along with her commentary. Is this earth-shattering content? Of course not. Did people follow along? Abso-fuckinglutely. Why? Because we can ALL relate.

The "boring" is what's going to create that sense of camaraderie and rapport with the eyeballs on you, and your elevated relatability is what's going to convert that camaraderie to trust, which, in turn, converts to sales.

HERE'S THE PART WHERE YOU ACTUALLY DO SOMETHING

Set a timer for two minutes and write out all the "boring" parts of your day today. To get things going, consider answering these questions:

- What did you have for breakfast?

- What chores or errands do you have to do today?

- What's the one seemingly mundane thing you look forward to the most all day? (For me, it's eating dessert after the kids go to bed.)

- What was the last topic of conversation between you and your spouse/partner/best friend/parent?

_____

_____

_____

_____

_____

_____

_____

BULLSHIT STORY #3: *I'm too fat*

Or *too ugly, too old, too dumb*. I often ask my audience of over 140,000 people what bullshit story keeps them from showing up on social media, and the amount of responses that relate to their physical appearance is overwhelming.

One of my biggest pet peeves is when I'm watching a woman on her Stories or a Live and she starts with an *apology* about *her appearance*. "Sorry, I'm such a mess . . ." or "Sorry about this huge zit on my face . . ." or "Sorry I didn't shower today, I'm so gross . . ." or "Sorry about this angle, I look so fat . . ." or "Sorry about that last Story, I'm so dumb . . ." (I used to do this, too, until my friend Shay called me out on it!)

Friends, the bullshit stories we tell ourselves about our looks being a hindrance to our ability to show up and connect with people may be the most painful of them all, but it's so relatable. We're our own harshest critics, and I'm not immune to it either. There are days (especially around my period) when I feel like the most disgusting, stupid, boring, uncreative person who's ever graced this planet. I'll look in the mirror and rip myself to shreds; my skin tone is uneven, my stomach isn't flat enough, my ass isn't fat enough, my short hair is ugly, I have no style. The abuse I'm able to put myself through before I've even technically started my day is astounding and, honestly, fucking exhausting. The fact that I show up every day makes me the Simone Biles of mental gymnastics. So when I tell you I get it, *I get it*. Here's the deal, though: no one is as concerned about you as *you* are. I'll never forget the one time I almost skipped a dinner date with my friends because I felt so embarrassed about the acne breakout I was having. It was all I could see when I looked in the mirror, and I didn't want to be seen by anyone or anything. I don't know what finally convinced me to get over myself and go to dinner, but one of the first things I said when I got there was, "I almost didn't come tonight because of this disgusting zit." My friend looked right at it and said, "I honestly wouldn't have even noticed it unless you pointed it out."

That's when I learned to stop creating mini billboards for every single insecurity I have. If I don't call attention to it, there's a really good chance no one will even notice. After spending over a decade sharing myself and my life on social media, I've realized we don't see ourselves the same way others see us. We see other people as whole beings—their energy, their smile, their sense of humor, and the way they make us feel. People perceive *you* the same way. So get your perfectly imperfect mug on social media and make some damn friends. While you're at it, just keep in mind that the number of likes you get on a post, views you get on a video, sales you get in a month, or revenue you make in a year do not define your worth as a human being. You are capable and deserving of all the success you desire. *Period.*

BULLSHIT STORY #4: *I'm too busy*

Despite what your mother may have led you to believe, you are not a unique snowflake. Everyone is busy, Buttercup, but the hard truth is that you're most likely too busy giving energy to the things that don't actually matter.

Hear me out.

Maybe you have a full-time nine-to-five job, kids, bills, or aging parents that you simply cannot ignore. Welcome to life. But things like saying "yes" to everyone and everything, watching TV for three hours a night, mindlessly scrolling TikTok whenever you find yourself with an iota of free time, allow energy vampires of humans and environments into your life. And all of this can take up so much space and make you feel like you're too busy to do the things that, yes, take effort but don't actually move the needle in your life and business. Remember that little part about discipline? That applies here.

Right this very moment, as I sit here writing this (well, actually, I'm on my walking pad at my standing desk—highly recommend), I feel *too busy* to be here in this moment. I'm trying to focus on the lessons I want to teach you and the examples I can give you to tie them in a pretty bow, but my mind is bouncing around like a frog on cocaine, leapfrogging between the things keeping me busy today. I have to call and reschedule the kids' dentist appointments before it's too late and we get charged for a late cancellation. I need to work out, switch the laundry over, and figure out how the hell to start an email workflow. I have seven unread texts that need responses, countless dirty dishes in the sink, twenty-five minutes until my first work call of the day, and two hours before I have to go pick up my youngest from preschool. That's what I need to do before noon, and I want those things off my list because they weigh on me, and I despise the feeling of a punch list hanging over my head. Today would be a great day to say, "I'll just get to my work later, when I have more time." But friends, I want to write a bestselling book that helps thousands of people, and the only way I can do that is if I create the time to complete the *actions* necessary to achieve my desired outcome. What I see people do, without even realizing it, is sacrifice what they want most for what they want *now*.

HERE'S THE PART WHERE YOU ACTUALLY DO SOMETHING

If this is your bullshit story, I want you to audit your day (honestly) tomorrow. Take out a piece of paper or whip out the notes section on your phone and list out the twenty-four hours you'll, God willing, be given tomorrow.

Take note of things like what time you *wake up* vs. the time you *actually get out of bed*. Do you hit the snooze button? Do you instinctively grab your phone, open social media, and scroll for fifteen minutes before you actually get up?

Take note of how many times you open non-essential apps on your phone and how long you're consumed by them. Social media scrolling minutes are like shopping at Ikea. *Oh, that's a cute little bowl for $3. That's a neat little whiteboard for my office for $7. That's a cool pillow I absolutely need for $12.* You walk all the way through that damn store, picking up "little things" here and there, only to get to the register and be slapped in the face with a $212 bill.

Our energy vampires are no different. A few minutes scrolling TikTok here, a few minutes reading celebrity gossip there, one YouTube video somewhere in between feels like nothing . . . but when you add up all of those "little things" throughout the day, you realize you spend a shit-ton of time busying yourself with things that don't really matter. Is all social media an energy vampire? Of course not. As someone who works many hours a week on social media, I have to be there. But there's a difference between getting on to check my DMs, respond to comments, and post my content VERSUS scrolling for no good reason (and yes, "inspiration" counts as "no good reason." Get out and live your life, and the content will be created for you, I promise). Am I saying that all scrolling on social media is bad? No, I'm not saying that, either. I love when I get to hang out there for a little while and consume content like the average person. (I think of it like happy hour with co-workers at the end of the day.) But there have absolutely been times where I've stayed for the equivalent of two too many drinks. Like, I should have gone to bed at 10:00, but I'm sitting there at the TikTok bar throwing back shots until midnight, knowing full well that my kids give zero fucks and will still wake up at the ass-crack of dawn despite how late *I* went to bed. As the saying goes, "everything in moderation." You have to identify your social media happy medium and stick to it. (For example, I have a timer on TikTok that kicks me off after I've spent a total of 90 minutes on it throughout the day. When that pops up, I know I'm done, and it's either time to go to bed or do something productive.)

LASTLY, FUCK THE FONTS

My friend Sarah is a creative director and brand strategist with over a decade of experience helping entrepreneurs discover their brand identities. We were having a conversation about this topic, the fear of being seen and known, and how it's not just about brand colors or the clothes you wear in your styled shoot. Truly leaning into this process of becoming *unafraid* of being yourself is a process of both unlearning and rediscovering oneself. Sarah was talking about how many times she's gone through this process with clients—hundreds of times—and most often, they get to what she calls the *fuck the font* stage.

After weeks and months of peeling back layers, getting uncomfortable, doing the hard work of creating a brand and image that feels truly aligned and authentic and on the verge of launching, the client will say something to Sarah, like, *Are we sure this is the right font for the website?* It's fear and control throwing one last Hail Mary (look at me with the football reference!) before you throw a middle finger in its face and decide to go for it. It's laughable, really, when you think that at the culmination of all this inner work, the last thing someone is going to fixate on is deciding between Helvetica and Arial.

HERE'S THE PART WHERE YOU ACTUALLY DO SOMETHING

What's your unique bullshit story that's been on replay in your mind for far too long?

Do you resonate with one (or more) of the examples from this section, or is it something different? The power of getting this bullshit story on paper and out of your head is so that you can see just how shitty and untrue it is. So, get it out, would ya?

Chapter 06

LEARNING TO LIVE OUTSIDE YOUR COMFORT ZONE

Now what about the roadblocks we set up for ourselves because we have the belief that if something feels uncomfortable it's bad? The conversations often go a little something like this:

You say: *I want to work for myself.*

Comfort says: *But do you <u>really</u>? You went to college to get a traditional job. Your parents have jobs. Jobs are what you know. Jobs are safe. You need insurance, and if you get it outside of your employer, it's wildly expensive. If you work for yourself, you'll never have any time to relax. It's probably more work than it's worth.*

You say: *I want to be well-known for what I do.*

Comfort says: *But do you <u>really</u>? Do you really want to risk people seeing you and judging what you're doing and saying? Think about the mean things said about well-known people. Internet trolls are brutal. I don't think you could handle that.*

You say: *I want the business that makes me one million dollars a year.*

Comfort says: *But do you <u>really</u>? Think about the taxes you'd have to pay on that. Be realistic; you didn't come from money, so money doesn't come to you. You should be grateful for what you already have. Think about what your family might think about you having all that money: greedy, selfish, superior. You know that you can't buy happiness.*

I know those are the conversations that happen because they're the ones I had with myself. I also know that they're lies because reality turned out to be much different.

Working for yourself is hard, sure. But it comes with the kind of freedom and flexibility that a traditional job could never give me. I absolutely work harder than I did when I worked a traditional job (my apologies to my former employers), but I work harder, and often at really weird-ass hours, because every single ounce of effort equates to my success. It also turns out you can buy insurance through the marketplace and be just fine.

Being well-known for your work can be scary as hell. People hiding behind screens say horrible things. But do you know what else is true? People on the internet can be absolutely amazing. I've met some of my closest, dearest friends through social media, and it's worth all the negative bullshit I have to navigate. Friends, you have to accept that if you want a lot of people to like you, you have to be okay with a lot of people *disliking* you. It's a tradeoff.

Creating a business that makes you millions of dollars is fun as hell. Taxes are a bitch, but I get this strange sense of pride and satisfaction that

I pay more in taxes than I ever came close to making as a salary when I was in the traditional corporate world.

Come to find out, not coming from money doesn't matter in regard to how much money you can make when you have a good idea and execute it. My family doesn't think I'm greedy or bad; they're proud of me.

So when I tell you that you have something of great value to share with the world, I need you to trust me more than you trust the comfort that's keeping you in a cage.

HERE'S THE PART WHERE YOU ACTUALLY DO SOMETHING

Take five minutes to freewrite about what your comfort is saying to you. Remember, this is a space where you don't have to worry about being logical, spelling things correctly, or being perfect. Just freaking get it out.

To help start the flow of things, consider these questions:

• What does your soul know to be true about what you desire?

_____

_____

_____

_____

_____

_____

- What is your comfort telling you?

_____

_____

_____

_____

_____

_____

- What do you want to say to your comfort?

_____

_____

_____

_____

_____

_____

- What might life look like if you gave comfort the middle finger and started listening to yourself?

FINANCIAL ROADBLOCKS

I met my husband during my first weekend at college, and from the start of our relationship, he's always been the numbers guy, I've always been the feelings gal, and never the twain shall meet. It's not unheard of for me to make a business (or life) decision based on a gut feeling. I trust energy and emotions and signs from the Universe, but I'm able to lean heavily into that side of myself because I've hooked myself a partner who is numbers- and data-driven. The problem comes when I want to make a decision that carries a significant financial investment, and I can only explain the ROI in *feelings*. Those conversations are the ones that make Cory's head explode, and I usually end up crying out of frustration for being misunderstood.

While numbers aren't my native language, I've come to appreciate how important they are when it comes to being a successful entrepreneur. As much as it pains me to admit, you can't simply bury your head in the ground and float on feelings and good vibes—you have to be able to make smart decisions when it comes to your money, and it's an area that often intimidates women (this is a generalization, of course) and causes problems.

LET'S TALK ABOUT DEBT

Until I was knee-deep into my entrepreneurial journey, I was led to believe that all debt is bad. But let's be clear: Not all debt is created equally. You taking on debt to buy a Ferrari *just because* isn't the same as taking on debt for the video equipment you need to start your event videography business. One is purely hedonistic, and one is an investment.

Depending on your business, you may have to go into debt for business startup costs or growth, and that causes many people to see red lights and stop signs. Many people don't understand that almost any business you'll start (whether it's your own business, a network marketing business, or something in between) will require some type of startup cost and regular overhead. When I started my career in network marketing, the startup investment was $1,000, and the thought of that made me want to vomit. We still didn't have an income after Cory lost his job, and I'd never considered any kind of debt outside my car, my student loans, and my mortgage. (Why? Because each of those felt like "safe" debt to me . . . whatever the fuck that means.) I almost didn't even take the idea to Cory because I was convinced he'd shoot it down in a heartbeat, and I'd find myself back at the drawing board trying to conjure up ideas for how I could make money from home while being a stay-at-home mom to two boys under two. Call it a nudge from the Universe, but I took the idea to Cory, and he said, "If you can take that $1,000 and turn it into something more, we'll never miss it." Desperate to make it "more," I went and dove in. In three weeks, I turned that $1,000 into $2,500, and over the next year, I turned it into an income that was more than what I was making full-time in the mental health field (and continued to do so for the next five years).

My best friend, Emily, has been very successful in the corporate world and owns her own stationery business, Faye Street Studios. (By the way, you should check out @fayestreetstudios on Instagram.) She runs the business from her home office and doesn't have any employees, but there were still startup costs involved in getting her business off the ground (as well as continuous overhead). Whether it was $300 to pay an accountant to set up her SCC and LLC applications or $5,000 for a fancy laser printer, a significant amount of money went (and continues to go) into creating and sustaining a business. The thing is, the laser printer has helped Emily create new offerings for her clients that have made her well over $5,000. When she bought the fancy machine, did she send me a text full of puke emojis? Yes. Did the investment make her a shit-ton of money? Also yes.

I have a client who is a hairstylist, and while she doesn't yet own her own salon, she rents a chair at one. Not only does she have the overhead of the monthly rent for the chair, but her startup costs came in the form of licensing and social media ads to build her client list. Were those investments scary when she put them on a credit card? Yes. Does she now have a massive client book and a six-figure business? Also yes.

Now here's where your inner critic might pop up from under her swampy bridge in the back of your mind and say, *But what if I can't make it into something more like they did?* You might start agreeing with this voice in your head, feeling like I might be a different breed than you, and you'll be tempted to stay exactly as you are in this very moment, rather than taking the chance on yourself by investing in your business. That's the opportunity cost of all of this. You can either make the investment and change, or you can stay safe and stay the same, but you can't possibly do both. When you think about it as a choice between evolving and staying the same, the price of the investment almost starts to feel insignificant. You're reading this book, so I know you don't want to be in the same place next year as you are now. (To be clear, I don't either!) So if a financial investment is keeping you from taking things to the next level, ask yourself what it will cost you if you *don't* take the leap. It won't always cost you money by not investing—it could be a dollar debt or a time deficit. For example, could I figure out how to make pretty graphics? Sure. Do I have the time to spend to do it? No, not really, because if I spent several hours trying to make a graphic, I couldn't spend those hours marketing, connecting, and selling (i.e., making money). So when it came time for me to upgrade the @noshamessalesgame account, it made sense to bring in help from people who actually know what they're doing (check out @ jointhesocialstudio, by the way—they did all my rebranding!) so I could stay in my zone of genius and not unproductively squander my time.

HERE'S THE PART WHERE YOU ACTUALLY DO SOMETHING

Get really real with yourself by answering these questions below either right here in the book or in your journal.

What is the biggest fear that's holding you back? Is it one that was listed here, or do you know deep down that it's something else?

Is there a financial roadblock that's currently in your way? If so, write down the investment along with three to five different ways you'll make a return on it.

Chapter 07

THE ANTI-HEY GIRL

UNDERSTANDING YOUR OPTIONS

Nowadays, Instagram (or Facebook, or TikTok . . .) is a place where average, everyday people like you and me can make some extra cash money.

Well, let me backtrack a little bit—the only way you don't fall into the "average, everyday people like you and me" category is if you're like my mom, and social media confuses you so much that you've used your Facebook status as what you thought was the search bar.

Ah, yes, on more than one occasion I've seen my mom's Facebook status as *Colleen Whitney Nichols*, to which I'll publicly reply, "You used your status again, Mom, but click my photo here and you'll be able to get to my profile and find whatever picture you were looking for to show Grandma." There's no shame if that's your social media speed, but maybe just stick to buying and selling household goods on Facebook Marketplace for the time being.

But everyone else, buckle up, because if you know how to even somewhat navigate social media (and/or have the desire to learn), you're sitting on a potential gold mine of seemingly endless possibilities.

TRADITIONAL NETWORK MARKETING VS. AFFILIATE MARKETING

If you don't follow me on Instagram (what the hell, by the way? Let's hang out @noshamesalesgame), you might not know that I consider just about everything on social media to be network marketing. Because when we hop on our social channel of choice and talk about a product or service that we like, what are we doing? Marketing to our (let's say it together, friends!) *network*.

Let me set the scene for you, dear reader. It's a great day; your kids are in school, you've got your iced coffee, your "nice" pair of black leggings, and you're ready to hit the club (and by *club*, I absolutely mean *Target*). While perusing the footwear, you stumble upon a pair of sandals that confuse you because, not only did you own them as a preteen, but they're being sold here, now? *What?* Excitement and glee flood your caffeinated bloodstream, and you throw those babies in the cart like the bad bitch that you are. Once you arrive home (and complete your sacred sit-in-your-driveway-and-scroll-your-phone-while-listening-to-the-same-songs-since-you-were-in-high-school time), you head inside and attempt a feet pic with your new shoes, which is humbling, because it's harder than it seems, but you're up for the challenge (and also confident you could never have an OnlyFans feet pic account). You finally snap the shot, and what do you do? *You post about them on your social media.* "Oh my gosh, I purchased a literal blast from the past today. #vintage." And what happens next? Someone slides into your DMs and says, "Oh my godddd! Where did you get those?! Send me the linkkkk!" And because goddesses don't gatekeep, you tell her you got them at Target, wearing them feels as if you're walking on clouds, and she *needs* them.

And *then* what happens? Your friend either goes to Target's website or heads to the store and buys them.

Congratulations, dear reader; you just marketed to your network and made a sale.

Except, *shit*, you don't get paid for it.

That's where traditional network marketing and affiliate marketing come into play. Now, I know that some people get really riled up about network marketing because they saw the LuLaRoe documentary or knew someone who knew someone who was in an MLM in 1995, only to end up with a garage full of products she never could sell. Are both of those things real? Sure. But it'd be like saying getting on the internet sucks because you once had to hear the AOL dial-up sound. It's outdated and rarely exists anymore. Modern-day network marketing and affiliate marketing are avenues that some people use to build a stream of income.

If you're someone who doesn't want to create their own offering (like a course) or provide a service (like a fitness coach), but you want to leverage your social media to make some money, network marketing or affiliate marketing programs might make the most sense for you.

These business models are strikingly similar, but let's point out the main differences.

DON'T MAKE IT WEIRD

1. Structure and Relationships

Network marketing: The network marketing option allows an individual to become an independent consultant who sells the company's products and makes a commission off not only their sales but also the sales of the people they bring into the company (*if* they choose to do so). This is what typically gets network marketing haters' panties in a tight wad. Is recruiting an option in network marketing? Yes. Can you still make money (and earn incentives) without recruiting a soul? Also yes. I know this because I've done it both ways at two different companies.

Affiliate marketing: Affiliate marketing is slightly different in that team building is not an option. It typically involves promoting and selling products or services on behalf of a company as an affiliate. Affiliates earn commissions based on their own referred sales or leads. The relationship is typically one-to-one between the affiliate and the company.

In both situations, you're essentially choosing a brand/product that you like, and you choose to talk about it on your social media, you share a unique link (given to you by the company), and you make a commission off any sales.

2. Compensation Model

Network marketing: Network marketers often earn both from their personal sales and the sales of their downline (key word: *often*). Team building is NOT necessary to earn money in network marketing, but it *is* the differentiating option. Network marketers may receive commissions based on the volume of sales within their network, and some companies offer additional bonuses or incentives based on team performance (I've earned several incredible all-expenses-paid vacations for my husband and myself, which is often no different than my friends in the corporate sales world!).

Affiliate marketing: Affiliates usually earn commissions on a per-sale or per-lead basis. The commission structure is generally straightforward, with predetermined rates or percentages for each successful referral.

3. Recruitment Focus

Network Marketing: Network marketing places emphasis on recruiting and building a team or downline, but I do see a shift in that trend slowly making its way through the industry. I see more and more companies focusing on and incentivizing sales over recruiting, which is a drastic change from even a few short years ago.

Affiliate Marketing: Affiliate marketing primarily focuses on driving traffic and generating sales or leads through various marketing channels. While affiliates can refer others to join affiliate programs, recruitment is not a central part of the business model.

4. Startup Costs

Network marketing: I like to think of network marketing as a business with training wheels; it's perfect for the person with the entrepreneurial spirit who wants to test the waters without going all in on costly startup costs like marketing, legal, shipping, insurance, etc. Now, of course, this is where the Karens and Chads like to come out with their virtual pitchforks and say, "It's a scam because it has sTaRt Up CoStS." To which I normally respond: "No shit, Chad, that's how business works." The start-up costs for a network marketing business can be as little as $45, with the average being in the $125 ballpark (of course, there are companies that cost more), and the monthly overhead is in the $49–$100 range if you decide to take the actual income-building route (as opposed to some people who join simply for the product discount and have no intention of selling anything for an additional stream of income). Since today's network marketing is focused on e-commerce, I highly discourage anyone from joining a network marketing company that requires you to carry and/or move inventory.

Affiliate marketing: Affiliate marketing typically has lower barriers to entry, with many programs allowing individuals to join for free. The main investment is the time and effort required for marketing activities, but let's not kid ourselves and pretend like that's free. Most professional and part-time affiliate marketers (a.k.a. influencers) spend money on the products they buy (to then recommend to their networks), ring lights, tripods, etc., not to mention the hours it takes to film the content for a thirty-second Reel or TikTok.

What about if you're neither of those things? You're an entrepreneur who has built their own product or service, and you want to start raking in those dolla dolla bills, y'all. Sweet. It's really no different—you're still showing up, connecting and engaging with, and eventually selling to your network. Be it real estate agents, personal trainers, coaches, finance experts, chiropractors, or underwater basket weavers, everyone who is selling something needs to be utilizing social media as a critical tool to grow their businesses.

MY EXPERIENCE WITH NETWORK MARKETING

In 2017, I was pissed off at the world. Cory had lost his job, I had to sell my dream home and take a *massive and humbling* downgrade, and my hormones were on the postpartum rollercoaster from hell. I didn't know how I was going to get my family out of this shithole of a situation, but I was determined as hell. Determined, but certainly not willing to fall for that "hey girl" MLM bullshit again . . . *right*?

Again, yes—because I had dipped (or, should I say, *stubbed*) my toe in the network marketing space not once, but twice before 2017. I had heard all the lines, dodged all the bullets, and *knew* (heavy on the sarcasm font there) that it wasn't for me. So you can imagine my utter rage and judgment when I saw this random Facebook friend posting about her "new business." She was happy, gorgeous, and doing the damn thing . . . and I *hated it*. And if I had been in a more emotionally healed state at the time, I would have simply unfollowed her and been none the wiser. But nay, friend, I was miserable in my life, so I need a good hate follow. (You know what I'm talking about—don't sit there all high and mighty like you've never been there, okay?) So, I didn't unfollow this chick—I watched her. Closely. And God, I wanted to hate all of her and all of it . . . but . . . I *couldn't*. My eye rolls quickly narrowed into genuine interest as I saw her begin to build this team of teachers, lawyers, nurses, hairdressers, and so many other educated, smart, professional women. *Is this not the stay-at-home-mom cult that I thought it was?* I would wonder to myself as I scrolled through picture after picture, Facebook Live after Facebook Live, thinking *If she can do this, I probably could, too*. But rather than doing anything, I'd mentally slap myself and talk myself out of it over and over and over again for months. Until one sleep-deprived night, I saw her post about how her paycheck from this little side gig was able to pay for all her Christmas presents for her two daughters that were the same ages as my two boys. *Fuck it*, I thought, and I sent her a message that said (quite literally): "Listen, are you #blessed for Facebook or are you actually making money with this side gig?" And not long after, I was telling her that I just wanted to make an extra $500 a month to help with groceries, and she was telling me that it was possible.

A few days later, I had signed up as a consultant, equal parts hating myself and excited that I might be able to actually do it this time. My game plan was to fly under the radar. I knew the negative things people thought of network marketing—because I *was* one of them. I remember my upline (the #blessed in real life Facebook friend who I'd never actually met in person) posting on Facebook that I had joined her team. She tagged me in her post, and I only knew about it because my best friend sent me a text with a screenshot of it and a message that said, "Are you fucking kidding me?"

I honestly feel nauseous just thinking back to that moment. I was so embarrassed for people to potentially see me try and fail yet again, and the thoughts of *Who the hell do you think you are?* pounded against every corner of my brain. Had I not been reading *You Are a Badass* by Jen Sincero (the book that changed my life, btw) at that exact moment, I think I would have folded. No shit. As I looked at that text and could hear my heartbeat in my ears, I had this crystal clear thought that can only be described as some sort of knowingness, and it was this: *People are going to watch, so you might as well succeed and give them a hell of a show.*

And that's what I've been doing with attraction marketing ever since.

Chapter 08

WTF IS ATTRACTION MARKETING?

So now that we've determined that you are, in fact, not too old or ugly or fat or stupid or boring to consistently show up on social media, how do you decide how to get people on social media to know you, let alone buy whatever it is that you're selling?

In-person networking events are equivalent to a payphone; they were super common at one time, and while they still exist, it's always a surprise when you see one out in the wild. As an entrepreneur in today's world, you have to master the social media game if you want to build a business and generate sales, and we do that by creating a magnetic social media presence.

When we think about creating a magnetic space on social media, we need to talk about the concept of attraction marketing. Before you started reading this book, had you ever heard of the concept of attraction marketing? When I typically ask this question to the groups I'm speaking to, it's a completely mixed bag. Some people study at the altar of social media strategy, and others are just happy to be able to find the Instagram app on their phone.

Regardless, I find most business owners have a skewed understanding of how attraction marketing actually works. Long story short, we're all a bit delusional.

We assume that if we talk about our business, product, or offering, people will automatically want to buy from us, as if posting to our feed and Stories is all it takes to rake in the sales. But listen, friend, none of us here is Selena Gomez. We don't have the luxury of hopping on our Stories and posting about our business only to have the floodgates open and billions of dollars flow into our accounts.

Attraction marketing—the concept of selling by *showing* your audience that they can't live without your product—is very real and not just for celebrities, *but it has to be earned*. More often than not, when I talk to entrepreneurs about this, they're frustrated, and they usually let out some exasperated sigh accompanied by something like, "I mean, I posted about it, and nothing happened. The algorithm sucks."

To which I reply, "Does the algorithm suck, or do you just have no idea how to connect with your audience?"

Normally, it's the latter.

THE ATTRACTION MARKETING EQUATION

For the average human who wants to use social media as a tool to grow their business and make money, we can break this down into what I call The Attraction Marketing Equation, or The Three C's: Content + Confidence + Consistency (= Money in the bank). Mastering this equation reminds me of what it was like when I was learning to drive. I had just gotten my learner's permit (after failing the test twice), and my mom let me drive home from the DMV. I was scared shitless, but equally excited by the fact that I was behind the wheel of an actual moving vehicle. Driving down Franconia Road in Alexandria, Virginia, was terrifying for me (and my mom, oh my God). It felt like so much to remember all at once—the turn signals, the speed limit, the staying in my own lane—shit, even reaching to turn down the radio felt like too much to handle. Some of my cousins lived up the street from us, and my mom suggested that we drive by and surprise everyone with who was actually able to pass the permit test. (I think bets were placed behind my back.) As we drove by, my cousin Daniel was in the front yard, and in a moment of excitement and not knowing what the hell I was doing, I tried to yell at him out the passenger window, point at myself, and look at him long enough to see his reaction. Thankfully, we were on a quiet neighborhood street because I absolutely swerved and missed a mailbox by a quarter of an inch. My mom, taking the Lord's name in vain, snapped me back to reality, and as I pulled into the driveway, I came to the conclusion that driving wasn't for me. How in the world would I ever be able to calmly check the rearview mirror and change lanes without shitting my pants? It was too much to learn, and it overwhelmed me. Today? I drive around with three wild banshees in the back, and I can hand out snacks, drink coffee, and talk on the phone all while my ears bleed from blasting CoComelon songs because God forbid my children listen to classic rock like the good Lord intended. Fifteen-year-old me would be shocked (and terribly embarrassed to know that we're jamming to "Wheels on the Bus").

Social media is no different. The first time I went live on Facebook, I had no idea what I was doing, and it took me fifteen minutes just to psych myself up enough to "go live." I didn't realize that it told you who was popping on to watch you, and I nearly had a heart attack when I saw an old boyfriend's name come up first. I didn't know where to look, what to say, or how to even post it to my feed once it was finished. I think maybe fifteen people watched it, and I was pretty positive I never wanted to do it ever again. Today? I'm on video nearly every day, and I am viewed by thousands of people. It's become second nature to me, and the concerns I used to have don't even come to mind. Much like with driving, I'm comfortable now because I've done it over and over and over again. So with this "equation," do your best to not get bogged down in the parts that feel difficult, unnatural, and foreign. It's not hard because you suck; it's hard because it's new. Mmkay? Let's get into it, shall we?

CREATING CONTENT THAT SELLS

The idea of content creation tends to intimidate people, but it's because "content" sounds jargony and official. In other words, it's simply deciding what you want to spend time talking about.

Here's the deal: If you wake up tomorrow morning, roll out of bed, look in the mirror and think, *Holy shit, I am a goddess walking amongst mere mortals . . . and I must document this with a selfie . . .* I hope you do.

I hope you find a window with natural lighting and take approximately forty-seven photos from thirteen different angles to get The Shot that captures your overwhelming beauty, and I hope you post it with gusto.

But I swear to all things good and holy, if you post that picture with a caption that says something like, *felt cute, might delete later* (paired with some dumb emoji . . .) I will have to fight the urge to hunt you down and throat punch you. Who does a caption like that actually serve?

Your ego, that's who.

All that's going to happen with that piece of content is that your besties will flood the comments section with fire emojis and YAS QUEENs and you'll get your dopamine hits while you sit back in your chair, smiling to yourself like the low-key con artist you are, thinking, *I know, girls. I know. I was never going to delete it.*

Listen, I'm not telling you to not post selfies or thirst traps or anything that highlights your overall badassery. What I AM telling you is that if you're going to post that selfie, give it some substance somewhere, please.

Pair it with a caption (or say on video) something along the lines of:

Finally, at 35, I'm feeling confident in my skin, and the more I think about it, I can attribute it to three key things:

1. *I've been prioritizing my sleep (goodbye, scrolling my phone for 2 hours in bed).*

2. *I'm drinking 100 ounces of water every day (hello, having to pee every 15 minutes).*

3. *I've been using these Unicorn Tears* consistently for the last 6 months and my mental health has never been better.*

What's something you do that helps you feel like your best self?

---

*In case you don't know me from @noshamesalesgame, Unicorn Tears is my universal term for the product or offering you sell.

What you're doing here is adding value by:

a. Talking about something of actual substance (feeling confident in your skin).

b. Giving recommendations (a.k.a. selling) two things that you don't actually "sell."

c. Recommending the thing you DO sell.

d. Creating a call to action in the form of **conversation**.

The typical equation (issue) I see countless social sellers make is the McMe scenario.

M: me

C: commercial

M: me

M: me

You're on social media talk, talk, talking about yourself.

Your kids. Your dog. Your latte. Your Bible.

Then WHAM, you throw in a weird-ass commercial about the one thing you sell. The vibe never lands, and people don't engage with, let alone *buy from*, you.

When the thing you "sell" is the ONLY thing you recommend that your audience buy, they see it as a commercial. And what do people do during commercials? They stop paying attention. Any of us who grew up in the '90s know that commercial time equals the opportunity to run to the kitchen and get a snack before *Boy Meets World* comes back on, and that's exactly what your audience is doing to you. They skip right past that shit, and they don't give it a second thought. It's a glaring money grab, and your audience feels zero connection to or investment in whatever it is that you're talking about.

When you're creating content for your social media, you need to ask yourself if it's **savable, relatable, shareable, or taggable**. Are you providing something like advice, a recipe, or a how-to that can be saved and referred back to? Is it relatable because you've let your guard down and are letting that freak flag of yours fly so that someone else can see it and think, "Oh gosh, me too!"? Might it be a combination of both of those things, so much so that people are heading to the comments section and tagging their best friends so they can laugh (or commiserate) together? If it can't fall under one of those categories, there's a good chance it belongs in your diary or in your therapist's office, not on your social media. Long gone are the days of cryptic lyrics from your favorite emo song, or a prayer request with no explanation, or a snapshot of your latte in a dimly lit cafe with a caption that says "vibes." Social media is so crowded and so fast that, to be relevant, you have to show up in ways that create engagement and intrigue from your audience.

> When you're creating content for your social media, you need to ask yourself if it's **savable, relatable, shareable, or taggable**.

When I look back at the origin of @noshamesalesgame, that account was nothing but pink and blue squares whipped up in a free app on my phone. I didn't think about brand colors, and my profile picture was a blurry screenshot of a unicorn from a Google image search (and stayed that way for nearly three years). The account didn't blow up at the rate it did because it was *pretty*; it grew at the rate it did because the *content was killer*. My Instagram account grew from zero to over 100,000 followers in one year *completely organically* because the content was sharable, savable, relatable, and taggable.

You can have the prettiest colors and the most thought-out brand, but if your content sucks, no one is going to stick around, and they're certainly not going to tell their networks to follow you. It's one thing to grip someone's eyeballs for half a second, but you're in a whole nother league if you can get them to *feel* something enough to then go and share it with their entire network. It was nearly a month after I started @noshamesalesgame that I realized I could see that people were sharing my posts. Cory and I sat there in shock as one post was shared hundreds of times. No one even knew (or cared) who I was, but I was saying things that struck a nerve with people *or* made them think, *Finally, someone is saying it*. Nearly six months after starting that account, I started selling community memberships, which was essentially my way of expanding on (and charging for) the free content I was creating on Instagram. With a membership site, I'm able to offer in-depth training, resources, and documents; invite guest speakers; and create a community of like-minded entrepreneurs who can network with and learn from one another. I was *floored* when we did $10,000 in business in our first month. *Once your content has people feeling something, sales become a natural byproduct.*

So how do we create a social media presence where selling feels like typical conversation? First, we have to figure out what your social media "channel" is all about, and what will make people excited to tune in to what you have to say.

CREATING YOUR CONTENT PILLARS

While everything you post on social media should be true and authentic, not every part of your life needs to be shared to create true and authentic rapport and relationships. To keep yourself from getting consistently tripped up in the "What do I talk about today?" spiral, we're going to create your content pillars. Your content pillars are the four to five overall topics that you generally talk about with your audience, and the good news is that identifying your unique content pillars is easy peasy lemon squeezy.

Here's what we're going to do: I want you to visualize going out to brunch with your best friend. You're there together with no time constraints, sitting on a patio somewhere cute and zero percent kid-friendly, you feel the sun on your skin in the perfect warm-but-not-sweaty way, you're catching up, and if you're like me and my best friend, maybe you've ordered some bottomless mimosas. When you think about being there with her, zoom out and consider the conversation that you're having. What are the four or five different things you'll talk about when you're together? Is it your family, the trash TV show you're both watching, the non-profit work you're doing, your fitness journey, etc.? Seriously, take some time and actually think about this. (And shit, if it's hard to do, what better reason to text your BFF and go to brunch?) Have your four to five things? Good.

HERE'S THE PART WHERE YOU ACTUALLY DO SOMETHING

Note your four or five content pillars here:

Pillar 1: _____

Pillar 2: _____

Pillar 3: _____

Pillar 4: _____

Pillar 5: _____

The other, arguably more critical, side of this visualization coin is identifying *how* you're talking about it with your best friend, in other words, identifying your *tone of voice.*

For example, one of the things I'd talk about is my family, but when I'm out with my best friend, I'm not going to be perfectly quaffed and concerned about every word that comes out of my mouth, and I'm certainly not going to bullshit her. I wouldn't say to my best friend, Emily, "Emily, I'm so hashtag blessed that Cory plays golf as much as humanly possible. I savor the solo time with the kids while he takes five hours to play outside, hitting a ball with a stick, because, you know, the days are long, but the years are short."

Fuck that.

I'm saying something more along the lines of, "Yeah, he's playing golf again tomorrow, and I have to figure out what the hell I'm going to do with the kids. Jesus, please, take the wheel . . . or send me a thunderstorm."

How you talk to your audience is equally important as what you're saying to them. Your tone of voice needs to become so recognizable that they know it's you from a mile away.

When I started @noshamesalesgame, it was completely anonymous. No one in my life, other than Cory, knew what I was doing. The account was growing quickly because people were sharing my posts left and right, and still, no one knew who the phantom "anti-hey girl" was (and that's the way I intended it to be forever!). It wasn't until a few months (and 40,000 followers) in, that my real-life friends started sending me @noshamesalesgame posts. "Have you seen this account?!" they'd ask. I'd answer honestly, "Yeah, I have!" and leave it at that. Then, my friends and acquaintances started sending them with more frequency and saying, "This person sounds *exactly* like you." (I probably used "douchebag" in a caption and gave myself away.) This is the power of leaning into your tone of voice and speaking like your genuine, authentic self. It will get to the point where it's so clear that people will know it's you (even if you're desperately trying to hide from them).

Your content pillars are meant to be guideposts, not concrete walls, and they can also change over time. The purpose is that when you have these guideposts in mind, it's easier to identify certain aspects of your life as conversation with your audience (a.k.a.: content).

For example, I have this low-key ability to connect with dead people. Like a medium. Fucking weird, I know. It's a very real part of my life, and often a guidepost for how I live, but it's not something I talk about on social media. I know it's a little (read: *very*) out there, and I know that the majority of my audience wouldn't connect with that part of me, so it's not a content pillar for my social media. That said, if I get a sign from my (very dead) dad, whom my audience knows about, I might mention it.

One of my content pillars is real-life motherhood because I get a kick out of sharing the real, raw (often hilarious) sides of being a mom, and that's something that most of my audience finds entertaining as well (even if they aren't parents). Knowing that, I always have at least half an antenna up, deciding if there are funny, relatable things that happen to me on any given day that I know my audience would enjoy. When I think of what to talk about on social media, I don't have to scan my *entire* day, just certain aspects of it. Having these content pillars, these guideposts, helps stop the overwhelm and analysis paralysis that so many of us have when it comes to creating content for social media.

HERE'S THE PART WHERE YOU ACTUALLY DO SOMETHING

Instead of hopping on camera and looking like a terrified toddler ready to burst into tears at a moment's notice, do yourself a solid and create a mental picture of who you're talking to. For me, I pretend like I'm on a FaceTime call with my best friend, Emily. I don't think about the thousands of strangers who will see me and potentially pick me apart, because when I do that, my voice goes up two octaves, and the people who know me in real life start sending me messages like "Blink twice if you're being held against your will."

List three people who make you feel at ease and who you feel like you can fly your freak flag in front of without concern. If you want to be a total badass and take this exercise to the next level, send each of these people a text and ask them to list their three favorite qualities about you. If you're anything like me, it feels easier to receive a box of explosives than a compliment, but I promise it's worth it. When you can get a glimpse into how other people who *truly know you* see you, it can help quell some of those bullshit stories we tell ourselves.

1. _____ makes me feel at ease. I trust their judgment, and, hey, they think I'm _____, _____, and _____.

2. _____ makes me feel at ease. I trust their judgment, and, hey, they think I'm _____, _____, and _____.

3. _____ makes me feel at ease. I trust their judgment, and, hey, they think I'm _____, _____, and _____.

ALLOW YOUR LIFE TO CREATE THE CONTENT

I grew up in a family where football Sunday was a *thing*. During football season, nothing else existed other than the Washington football team (and church). The issue? I hate football. I don't understand a lick of it, and if we're being honest, it's probably where I developed trust issues. (Can someone explain to me how three minutes on a football clock equates to thirty minutes in real life?!) On these days, there was never any deviation from The Plan. My mother, who otherwise lacked any sort of ability to make herself and her enjoyment a priority, ruled with an iron self-care fist on Sundays. She would drag me and my brother to 8:45 Mass, and then we'd come home and wait for the game to start.

Looking back now, as a mom of three young boys, I can only imagine how fucking annoying I was, pouting and complaining about being bored all damn day when my mom wanted this *one thing* for herself. To her credit, she gave no shits. "Figure it out," she'd say. And oftentimes, that resulted in me sitting in my room, writing in my journals about how hard and *unfair* a life I was forced to live (cue the eye rolls), only coming out to enjoy the one silver lining of *the football*: snacks.

Alas, the struggle continues. Much to my disappointment, my husband is also a raging football fanatic.

One of the first times I hung out with Cory outside of a dark, beer-soaked frat party was when he invited me over to his apartment one Sunday to . . . watch football. I was so mad at myself for leaning hard into playing the cool girl card. *Why did I let that Cosmo magazine quiz convince me that this was the best plan of action?!* Before he came to pick me up, I called my mom in a panic. "I need to know about football. What should I say?" She was half appalled, half excited. Appalled that I had spent eighteen years of my life sitting with her on Sundays and couldn't even *pretend* to know anything about the game, excited because she thought, *Maybe she'll end up liking sports for this guy.* (Spoiler alert: that did not happen.)

Weeks passed, and after I felt like I had this whole dating thing in the bag, I told Cory that I couldn't live the lie anymore. The Irish-Catholic guilt was eating me alive. I confessed that I didn't know what a first down was, that my mom fed me one-liners before we hung out on Sundays, and that I only knew when to cheer because I pay attention to social cues. I conceded that I hated football, and if we never watched it again, it would be too soon.

How he worked past his devastation, I'm still not sure.

But fast-forward fifteen years, and football finally did me a solid.

On a random Sunday afternoon during football season in 2021, the familiar feelings of loathing and random rage directed at a ball made of pigskin crept in. By now, with three kids, I couldn't retreat to my room for four hours and write in my journal, and I sure as hell wasn't going to pretend to be interested to impress Cory. So what else was an elder millennial to do in this time of despair? Hop on Instagram, of course. I bid my hellos to my fellow football-hating wives and simply asked a question to stir up the conversation that I certainly wasn't having at home that afternoon. I talked about how I grew up with a mom who would often yell so passionately at the TV on football Sundays that our neighbors could hear her. That, ladies and gentlemen, is not normal.

So I asked, "What's something that you thought was normal when you were growing up but then realized as an adult that it wasn't?"

At first, silly submissions came in: peanut butter on pancakes; calling eggs over easy "dippy" eggs; not having your Christmas presents wrapped on Christmas morning. I shared them, adding my own commentary along the way, happily distracted during the game (and yes, *gasp!* Sometimes I'm on my phone in front of my kids). Then, something out of left field found its way into the question box: *"We had a poop knife."*

A *what the fuck* knife?!

I was flabbergasted, confused, and genuinely curious. I shared the response with the crowd, and they shared in the WTF-ness of it all. And then Poop Knife Girl slid into my DMs, explaining that a poop knife is exactly what you'd think it is—a knife to chop any logs that might be too girthy to flush.

With my mouth agape, I shared this discovery with my audience. *Has anyone else ever heard of such a thing?!* I wanted to know. And thus, I spent the next several hours discussing this not only in my DMs but in my Stories as well. It was such a great conversation that I *saved it as a Highlight* on my Instagram (@colleen__nichols).

If you're reading this and thinking, *Why the hell are you telling me about a feces utensil?* I promise I'm getting to the point.

Not only did this create a massive conversation and a sense of camaraderie with my audience, but it also sparked the idea of what I now call "Question Box Sunday." Every Sunday, I take to my Stories and ask wild, provocative questions, people spill the tea, and I get to build trust with my community.

People who hang out with me on social media often tell me that I know more secrets than a Catholic priest, and while I don't regularly compare notes with clergymen, I think they may be right. My audience tells me *everything*. I know about their sex lives and what kinds of kinks they're into, they share family secrets and some of the most intimate details of their private lives, and I know what random anxieties plague them. I know what medications they're on, what "work" they've had done, and who's cheating on their partners. The reason that people are so honest with me is because they trust me because I've put years of emotional equity into creating a space that makes them feel free to share without shame or judgment.

And all of this spawned from being bored on one of my least favorite days of the year. I didn't think it through. There was no "agenda" to be had. I honestly wasn't even sure if anyone would play along. But, boy, did they ever! This is a shining example of how you don't always need an "engagement strategy" or some formula to create the audience engagement of your dreams.

I have the utmost trust from my audience, and because of that, I'm able to sell them anything. But keep in mind that that trust and rapport weren't built on things even remotely related to something I sell. It was built on human interaction. I do use it to my advantage, though. Because I know my insights will be highest on Sundays and Mondays, I usually recommend (a.k.a. sell) something in my Stories on Monday mornings that I know my audience will enjoy. It should come as no surprise that my sales do quite well on Mondays.

If this were a speech and not a book, I'd ask everyone who feels the need for a content calendar to raise their hands. All of you type A freaks would raise your hands and gush over how you can't live without a schedule and that you feel like a ship lost at sea without a list of all the things you need, want, and "should do" on a daily basis. While my brain doesn't work the same as my type A friends', the crazy in me recognizes the crazy in you. I understand that some people rely on a calendar or schedule when it comes to content creation; otherwise, they freeze up and take zero action. My caution to the content calendar lover is this: don't let your plan get in the way of magic. Your life is going to provide you with so many opportunities for content creation that you'll miss it if you're hyper-focused on Motivation Monday, Tasty Tuesday, Wellness Wednesday, and so forth. There will also come a Monday where you have no motivation to fake, a Tuesday when you're grabbing Chick-fil-A instead of making a tasty home-cooked meal, and a Wednesday when you do more cussing than meditating. When those things happen to the calendar queens, they struggle with thinking outside the box.

THE THREE S'S: SELF, SOCIAL PROOF, SELL

So instead of writing a weekly schedule in stone, work with a rough outline. Take a look at your calendar and first see if there's anything time-sensitive that you need to plan around. Do you have a sale coming up? Are you rolling out a new product or offering? Are there any shopping holidays around the corner?

Then, I want you to look around your house, your recent Amazon orders, or your bank statement and pick three things you've spent money on in the last week or so. Take note of them, and at some point during the week, tell your community on social media if you recommend it or not (and *why*). Thirdly, you're going to pick one product or offering of yours that you want to sell (if you only sell one product or offering, pick a specific aspect of said product or offering) and figure out three different ways to talk about it.

This is your content outline for the week.

If I were to follow this outline (and not fly by the seat of my pants like I normally do), my real-life example would be:

Calendar:

Valentine's Day is two weeks away, so maybe I'll do a promotion teaser this week about buying DSGC for someone you love.

Recent purchases:

- A purse off Amazon
- New glasses from Warby Parker
- Air Force 1s.

I would not recommend the purse because the color is different from the way it looked online and it's bulky. I'd show it to my community, and I'd do a side-by-side of "what I ordered vs. what I got." I would talk about how I'm looking for a mid-sized bag that can also be worn cross-body (and for bonus engagement points, I'll ask for recommendations). Without fail, the DMs will come pouring in as my internet friends agree that I was catfished by a purse, and they'll send me links to their favorites.

Later in the week, I'll absolutely recommend the glasses I got at Warby Parker, because they're cute as hell and I bought two pairs for a fraction of the cost of one pair at my eye doctor (and I'll add the link to the glasses

I bought). I'll ask my community who out there wears glasses and where they buy them from. I'll put up a question box and share some popular answers with the rest of the group.

I'll give a mixed review of my Air Force 1s. I was influenced, but I'm not sure I love how they feel. The high-top fit isn't something I'm used to wearing (and I'll ask my audience if they know if they're more comfortable once I break them in). Sticking to my natural flow of content, I'll talk about being a millennial who is caught in a love triangle with her skinny jeans and wanting to actually look cool. This opens the door for dialogue because I know that most of my audience falls in the "millennial" range, and that this is a super common *situation* for us. We'll commiserate, laugh, share favorite fashion influencer accounts, and before you know it, people will be sending me millennial memes out of the blue.

Talking About a Product Three Ways:

I sell a product on my personal social media and an offering on @ noshamesalesgame, so let's look at those two examples.

The best equation for talking about one product three ways is the Three S's: self, social proof, sell. Here's an example of how I would apply the Three S's to the CBD gummies I sell.

> **Self:** I'll talk about mental health and normalizing taking medication when you need it. This falls in line with my content pillars, and it's a topic of discussion that my audience has come to expect from me. I'll show my Prozac pill and a CBD gummy, I'll talk about how they make me feel, and I'll add the link. For

the rest of the day, I'll field DMs about mental health, medication, and CBD. Never once in these conversations will I say something like, "Well, Melissa, it sounds like you really should buy these gummies." Hell no. Melissa is talking to me about something extremely vulnerable: her mental health. It would be inappropriate to turn that conversation into a sale. Melissa may ask about the gummies, and in that case, we'll talk about them! But I won't use her vulnerability as a bait and switch. Without fail, though, someone else will come into my DMs and say something like, "Okay, give me the link, I need those gummies." Of course, I'll send the link and tell them to send any questions they have my way and that I'd be happy to help. This creates a low-pressure environment, and they know I won't hound them for a sale. Because I've made this person feel safe, they will absolutely ask me questions and engage with me. When people are ready to buy, they buy. It's my job to continually remind them that a) I'm a human being, and b) I like a certain product because it helps with my mental health.

Social proof: I'll share a screenshot of a text or DM from a customer giving their feedback about what they think about the gummies, and I'll add the link again, telling people if they're ready, here's where you can get 'em. If you don't yet have people randomly sending you testimonials, that's fine! You can create this type of social proof by asking customers how their experience has been, or by saying something in your Stories on your "self" day like, "I know I'm not the only one whose life has been changed by these bad boys." That cues people to give you their off-the-cuff testimonial. I treat my DMs like a vault, and I also share tons of things that are said there. It's imperative that when I share something that's been said in my DMs or texts, I screenshot it and share it in a way that keeps the person anonymous. If the message has identifying information in it (i.e., a family member's name) I either blur it out or ask the sender for their permission to share it. A pro tip: save all your screenshots like this to a "social proof" folder in your photos. There's no reason why you can't use them again later!

Sell: I'll talk about how, as a mom, I sometimes experience sensory overload. Kids screaming, touching me, and asking me a million questions *sometimes* grates on my nerves. I'll swear to my community (genuinely) that these gummies help calm me so that I'm not a grumpy, snappy version of myself. I'll say, "If anyone can relate to that feeling, you need to buy these things now and thank me later." I'll add a link and call it a day. Some people will click the link and buy what I'm selling. Others will DM me and chat about how their kids' whining grates on their nerves, too! Both are wins in my world because I'm either making money or making genuine connections.

What if you share a service and not a product? Cool, I do that, too. I also sell a service, a membership to Direct Sales Growth Community (DSGC). Here's how we'd apply the Three S's to that.

Self: I'll talk about how I just got off my favorite weekly call inside of DSGC, Office Hour. I'll talk about how I love the group coaching/mastermind feel that it has, and how so many ah-ha moments happen for members during this call. I'll add a link, directing people to click it if they wanted to join in on the next Office Hour call. I often then add a slide where I put up a question box and tell people to drop their business questions, and I'll answer a handful of them throughout the day. Not only is this providing free value to my audience, but it also gives them a sample of my coaching style and overall knowledge, which helps them decide if spending their money with me feels like a good fit.

Social proof: Fortunately, I have the best members in the entire world who are always so generous with their words, taking the time out of their days to randomly send me DMs about how DSGC is impacting their lives and businesses. (I truly cherish every single message!) I have a folder in my photos where I save testimonials like this to share every week (and to read when my mindset is in the gutter and I'm feeling like a failure!). I've also created a Highlight titled *Proof* where I often save testimonials, and at the <u>end of every feed post</u> I make, I tell people to check it out.

Sell: I'll talk directly to my target customer, the entrepreneur who wants to do sales on social media the right way. I'll talk about popular (yet antiquated) techniques that now just give people the ick, and I'll tell them the solution I have readily available for them. I'll tell them that when they're ready, I have the link.

ELEVATED RELATABILITY

When it comes to attraction marketing and being a human on the internet, it's about being freaking relatable, right? Like we talked about earlier, there's no need to create a perfect, untouchable social media façade when, in reality, you take a morning dump just like everyone else. But where's the line between being relatable and people being concerned about you vs. being relatable and people wanting to hang out with you? It lies in the art form of elevated relatability, the concept that you want to share whatever human experience you're going through, but not when you're swirling around in the eye of the storm. You want to come from that viewpoint of being still close enough that you can relate to all the nitty-gritty details, but also having just enough distance from them to see things a little more clearly than the person who's still being tossed around in the waves.

For example, I talk a great deal about mental health on my personal Instagram. Not because my education is in mental health, but because I have lived with anxiety my entire life. I know what it's like to have that voice in your head turn every simple, calm moment into a super fun game of *What If This Tragic Thing Happened.* I know what it's like to spend the majority of your life battling with body dysmorphia, desperate to see yourself through anyone's eyes but your own. I know what it's like to battle with disordered eating, because the calories you consume are the only things you feel like you can control in your life. I know what it's like to take the long way because the route that makes the most "sense" has an intersection that you don't like. I know what it's like to self-sabotage over and over and over again. I know what it's like to be the best version of yourself on medication. I know what it's like to be broke as a joke and to feel suffocated by the crushing weight of debt and the toll that takes on your mental health. I also know that I'm not alone in any of that.

So I talk about it.

On the days when I bring in some aspect of mental health, I know I'll need to triple the amount of time I typically spend in my DMs—because it's one of those topics that so many people can talk about but so few do (because anxiety is a little bitch).

Do I show up on social media when I'm in the middle of an anxiety spiral? *No.* But the next day, when I realize that it was anxiety and not a heart attack, or a stress headache and not a brain tumor, I hop on and talk about it. I talk about it because it forges a real, genuine connection with my community on social media.

I don't talk about my anxiety in my DMs with someone and have "make them a customer" on the back burner of my mind. Absolutely not. My goal with social media, always, is to connect first and sell second. If I can connect with someone about something like anxiety, and they feel safe talking to me about their life, I don't have to worry about selling, ever. Because if I have that connection, I know that sales will be a natural byproduct. I know that when I'm in my Stories or on social media talking about the things I do sell, they're already paying attention, and they already trust what I'm telling them. There's absolutely no need to chase or hound anyone, because when it's a good fit for them, they come to me. They do that because they consider me to be a human just like them, not some untouchable avatar.

Chapter 09

HAVE A DAMN OPINION

THE SECRET WEAPONS OF ENGAGEMENT

There are two other crucial concepts you can implement that make your content wildly engaging: asking for suggestions and giving recommendations.

Listen to me; people love nothing more than to give their opinion about anything and everything. We love to feel helpful, and if sending a link or giving you my two cents will do it, I'll be in your DMs like it's my damn job.

A pro tip? If you're going to Google it, you should be hopping on your Stories or channel of choice and having a conversation about it with your audience (unless, of course, you're Googling something like "Is this chlamydia?")

Say you're a thirty-five-year-old woman whose body has birthed three children, kinda shows it, and whose wardrobe consists of "good" leggings and "house" leggings. If you find yourself befuddled and confused by today's fashion, talking to your channel of choice would be a good idea.

As you may have guessed, this is not a hypothetical situation. It's me, hi. And you can bet your bippy I took to my Instagram Stories and leaned into my audience for help.

"I mean, Jesus Christ, what am I even supposed to be wearing these days? I want to find shorts that don't look like they'd give me a yeast infection, but I also don't want to look like I shop at the same establishment as my grandmother. HELP A SISTER OUT."

And wouldn't ya know it, all the Recommendation Ritas came out of the woodwork, selflessly sending me links to their beloved pairs of denim shorts, oftentimes accompanied by their own glowing reviews. In other words, they were *selling* to me.

By taking my genuine confusion about fashion to my audience, I normalized what it is to sell, to send links, and to give testimonials. So guess what? When I'm the one giving recommendations and posting links, we've already established that this is what friends do with one another. It's the same thing in real life, too. My friend, Shauna, and I were on a girls' trip and had the fun idea to create a masterclass about making sales fun, because over lunch, we *naturally* recommended so many things to each other. She told me about the lip gloss she loves, and she pulled out her phone and sent me the link. I told her about the ice roller for my face I just bought off Amazon, so I pulled out my phone and sent her the link. Back at the hotel room, we sampled each other's skin care lotions and potions, swapped sleep hygiene tips, and shared business investments we'd recently made. It was *all* selling, but without any ick. The truth is, we trust our friends more than advertisements, and when one of our friends gives a product or service their stamp of approval, we're all but ready to throw our credit card at it. Being a friend on social media is no different, which is why it's critical that you position yourself as someone who makes solid recommendations. Because if they buy the lip gloss you recommended and they end up loving it, or if they buy the ice roller off Amazon and love it, they won't think twice about buying *your* product and loving it.

The impact of regularly asking your audience for their recommendations is twofold. Not only will you normalize selling, but their presence in your DMs or comments is telling the algorithm gods that Suzie Q likes your content so much that she interacts with it, and when she interacts with it, she's on the app longer, and because *your* content keeps *her* on the app longer, they'll make sure that your content is some of the first that she sees every time she opens the app. So today you may be talking about shorts, but tomorrow you may be talking about your business, and Suzie Q is more likely to see it because she spent time talking to you about denim shorts.

The other side of this coin is *giving recommendations*. I want you "selling" things that you don't actually sell (meaning, making a commission from). I want you to tell your audience about the lip gloss you're wearing, where you got your shirt, why this certain lint roller is the best, and why everyone needs to watch whatever show you're watching.

Why? Because doing so makes them see you as a valued recommendation resource, and they're not subconsciously repelled by you "selling."

I am constantly telling my audience about most of my purchases, and I'm linking to things I love every damn day. I genuinely want them to know about the things I use and love, and I also want them to trust me. If they end up buying the lip gloss from CVS or the shirt from Amazon or the lint roller from the best lint roller manufacturer, and like them as much as I do, they won't bat an eye when I share the thing I actually make a living selling. If they trust me enough to open their wallet for the shirt I'm wearing, they're much less likely to balk at, or even question, the thing I make a commission from talking about. I recently had someone in my DMs jokingly say, "Damn it, Colleen, I need to stop watching your Stories because I spend money every time I'm here." What a compliment! And what a testimonial that making consistent recommendations gets my audience to spend more money with me.

One of the biggest mistakes I see people make online is trying to be liked by everyone. While on that impossible pursuit, they lose any kind of magnetism. They become a forgettable beige wall that everyone walks past and pays no attention to. Even if you're as vanilla as they come, I need you to add some motherfucking sprinkles.

PURPOSEFULLY POLARIZING

This is where the idea of being purposefully polarizing comes into play. I first heard this phrase from Lauren Chamberlain (when she gave a training in Direct Sales Growth Community), and it was validating to have an actual phrase to describe what I'd been spending the last decade doing on social media.

I know many of you are clutching your pearls at the sight of the word **polarizing** and you skipped right over the strategic word: *purposefully*. If you want people talking to you and engaging with your content, you've *got* to have some opinions.

Now, this doesn't mean I need to know who you voted for, how you feel about vaccines, or what chemicals in food you think are killing people (those topics are all absolutely fair game, but for *most people*, that's stepping outside of their comfort zone and into their panic zone). The great news is that being polarizing doesn't mean you have to be divisive. It simply means you're taking a stance on something, *anything*. For example:

Starbucks is superior to Dunkin'.

Coke is better than Pepsi.

Chocolate is better than sour candy.

Apples are better than oranges.

(I would say these are things that won't offend anyone, but it's social media. People can be offended by *anything*. I can absolutely see someone coming into your DMs like, "Um, what you said about oranges is really offen-sav. My mom used to work for an orange farm, and apples are super toxic." Get outta here with that, Susan. Ain't nobody got time to be bogged down by petty shit.) The point is, making a statement simply gets people talking to you. And when you get people talking to you, the algorithm gods take note that your content keeps Suzie Q on their app, so they'll make sure to feed her your stuff first every time she logs on.

An example that comes to mind is when, during a video training I did in DSGC, I was talking about being purposefully polarizing, and I gave a festive example, as we were at the end of October. In the training, I gave an example from my own Stories of how I was talking with my Instagram community about Halloween candy. In this training, I casually mentioned that the comment I made was: Reese's shapes (like a pumpkin or Christmas tree) taste way better than the normal circle Reese's. Well, wouldn't ya know it, I got on Instagram later that morning, and my good friend Sara Moon is in *her* Stories talking about *my* training and my alleged mispronunciation of the word "Reese's."

According to Sara, it is pronounced REEC-IZ. Hearing it made my skin crawl. Pronouncing it Sara's way felt like knives on the tongue. It couldn't be right. Obviously, the correct way to say it is REE-SEES.

So, of course, I shared her Story (and my opinion). Over the next twenty-four hours, my DMs were *ablaze*—people felt some kinda way about the pronunciation of this chocolate candy. People from Team Sara were sending me articles and YouTube videos. People from Team Correct—I mean *Colleen*—were sending me passionate voice clips and DMs telling me how right I was. People were getting on *their* Stories and talking about how *they* pronounce it, and they were tagging Sara and me. It was lighthearted, well-meaning, and *funny*. It also resulted in new followers, high engagement, and a way to build rapport with people who were hanging out in my corner of the internet. Although it was unexpected, I knew that the following day, as I wrapped up the candy debate and still had lots of eyes on me, that I'd strategically talk about the product I sell. I said, "I'm taking some extra CBD today because I'm a little anxious about how many *REEC-IZ* psychopaths are out there roaming around." It came as no surprise to me that I had an influx of orders that day. People had come to my channel, had a positive experience, and as such, felt more inclined to make a purchase based on a recommendation I made.

The same thing happened recently when I was on a JetBlue flight. As the kid of a flight attendant, I rarely pay attention to any announcements (sorry), but this time I just so happened to pull out my AirPod and listen. The flight attendant told the plane that we were going to play a game. She was going to ask a question, and if you knew the answer, you were to press the flight attendant call button so it would light up. I can't remember the trivia question she asked, but people were *into it*. Hands were flying up, lights were going off, and people were laughing. The flight attendant went on to ask a series of three trivia questions, and then she started talking about the airline credit card that she would be passing out if anyone was interested. Having a mother who used to do the same thing, I knew that she would get a cash bonus for every credit card that was opened. As she walked down the aisle, I saw a significant number of passengers taking the pamphlet from her. Would every single person who took a pamphlet end up opening a credit card? Of course not. But it's a numbers game. What that flight attendant did was a simple, yet brilliant, example of how important it is to get your audience's attention and engagement before you try to sell them something.

Celebrities who go on talk shows are no different. The whole purpose of a celebrity going on a talk show is to promote a project that's getting ready to launch—whether it's a new movie or (yet another) tequila brand, the celebrities are there to sell the shit out of something.

Julia Roberts and George Clooney had a new movie come out a few months ago, and I happened to see an interview with them that highlighted this perfectly. The two came out, and the host asked them about their decades-long friendship, the pranks that George has played on Julia, and a handful of other rapport-building facts. They then played a silly game where Julia was blindfolded and had to touch the faces of several men and guess which one was George. After spending time humanizing these actors and making the audience laugh, they found their way back to the host's couch, and he held up a picture of their new movie. They gave a thirty-second synopsis of the film, a thirty-second clip played, and it was wrapped up by the host telling the audience when they could go see the movie.

Most of their time in front of the audience was spent building rapport, having a sense of humor, and reminding people that *stars, they're just like us!* THEN they sold. This is the kind of cadence that your social media needs to adopt for you to be successful at online sales. Your content should be a four to one personal-to-business ratio.

HERE'S THE PART WHERE YOU ACTUALLY DO SOMETHING

When it comes to creating content, you need to make it crystal clear who you're talking to every time you write a post or hop on video. **If you try to be for everyone, you'll end up being for no one.** Don't worry about "excluding" people, because when you're clear on who you're talking to, the right people will always show up, even if they're not the avatar you've created. For example, I follow several fitness accounts. I am not, nor will I ever be, a fitness enthusiast, but I get really good ideas from them about certain recipes and workout tips (that I may or may not ever implement, but I enjoy pretending I will). I'm not the target audience for these creators, but I stick around because they nail their content every single time. They know who they're talking to and why. They're not talking to a semi-couch potato like me; they're talking to people who get hyped up to lift heavy things and run for enjoyment. They don't have to worry about "excluding" me, because they're so clear on *who* they're talking to and *why*, that someone like me can follow along and still get value from their content.

Get out a journal and freewrite to answer any or all of these questions:

- Who are you talking to when you hop on social media? Create this person in your head, for real.

  - Are they male? Female? Non-binary? Transgender?

  - How old are they?

  - What is their sense of humor like?

- What's their biggest area for growth?
- How does this person feel after consuming your content?

- What makes your content different from your peers' content?

_____

_____

_____

_____

_____

_____

_____

_____

_____

_____

_____

_____

_____

_____

- How are you adding value?

- Make a list of the last thirty things you purchased. (Now you have something to recommend every day for the next month.)

- Make a list of thirty things you're curious about. (Now you have something to ask your audience every day for the next month.)

- What human characteristics connect you with other people on your social media?

Chapter 10

BE A
BONFIRE

No matter how long you've been in business, people have to warm up to whatever it is you're doing. We have two ways to imagine this. Scenario one: you're a warm little campfire, surrounded by a family of four who are roasting marshmallows and creating core memories. While lovely, it's unlikely that anyone is going to tap you on the shoulder and ask if they can join you.

The second scenario is this: WOOSH—you're a big-ass bonfire. Burning Man style. And while I'm not into dancing around a burning flame while partaking in psychedelic drugs, that shit is bound to catch people's attention. At first, people may watch you from far away, assuming that the bonfire isn't for them. But when you show up day after day, with the energy of someone who cannot be fucked with, they're going to take a closer look.

I need you to be that bonfire.

Here's the secret: **people will buy your confidence first and your product second.**

When I started a social selling business, the only thing I had to stand on was a pile of failures. I tried to start a business when I was in grad school, and come to find out, I was too chickenshit to talk to people. Then, as a newlywed, I wanted to flex that entrepreneurial muscle for a second time, only to strike out yet again because I was shocked that you had to be consistent. The third time, years later, I found myself yet again wanting to scratch that entrepreneurial itch . . . but so terribly wrapped up in my own bullshit stories.

What will people think of me?

I'm not a businessperson.

I'm not good at sales.

What if everyone watches me fail? Again.

And as if the Universe herself were answering me, I heard it clear as day: *What if you decide to succeed and give them a good show?*

That got my wheels spinning faster than I could keep up, and it fueled a new purpose within me. I realized that people *were* going to watch me (because that's the very nature of social media), and I knew that some of them were going to judge me no matter what. And that's when I decided to make my own bonfire of sorts: my Fuck You Fire.

> Here's the secret: **people will buy your confidence first and your product second.**

Any time I was concerned with what someone would think of me, or when someone made a snarky remark about my "little business," I would accept it as fuel and dance like a maniac as I threw it into the flame of my Fuck You Fire.

In my first month in business, with zero clout to stand on, I had four people join my team and I did over $5,000 in sales. It wasn't because I had gotten elite training or taken a sales course; it was because I decided to show up with the kind of confidence that people couldn't fuck with.

The thing is, we all have that somewhere within ourselves. If you're anything like I was back then, you may have to dig *really deep* to find it, but I promise you it's there. A little trick I like to use when it feels like all the confidence has been drained from my being is to remember a time in my life when I *did* feel confident.

For you, maybe it was that time you won the spelling bee in third grade. Maybe it was the time your boss complimented the project you'd presented. Maybe it was when you advocated for someone and ended up making a difference. The thing is, your brain doesn't know the difference between current reality and a memory—is that not wild as hell?! *You can literally borrow confidence from your memory.* So the next time you feel fear and insecurity creeping in, rewind your brain and find any moment in the history of your life that you felt like a badass, and go do the damn thing.

The first several times I got on live video, I was petrified. As in, *could-only-wear-black-tops-because-I-had-pit-stains* petrified. Although it's second nature to me now, back then, it was a terrifying idea that I wanted to avoid like the plague. I'd spend nearly thirty minutes hyping myself up and practicing what I was going to say, but the more I did it, the easier it became. I'm not special, so the same thing will happen for you.

While I'm not someone you'd consider to be particularly fit (at all), I often compare sales techniques with going to the gym. If you're a virgin gym goer, it's terrifying to step foot into the gym for the first time. You have no idea where to go or what to do with your hands. When you do eventually end up lifting weights, those puppies are heavy as hell. You're sore afterwards—both your muscles and ego feel a bit bruised. But then you go back again and again and again, and not only do you figure out where to go and what to do with your hands, the weight starts to feel easier to pick up.

Showing up on social media is no different. It's scary, intimidating, and can feel super confusing. You overthink how people are perceiving you, and you often leave feeling a little bit insecure about how you showed up. But the next day is easier, the weight becomes lighter, and you start making real progress. But again, I know it can feel overwhelming and in-timidating. Deciding to show up in a consistent, authentic way on social media will absolutely require a bit of resilience.

ON RESILIENCE: DOWNRIGHT AWFUL VS. SEVERELY INCONVENIENT

So let's get this straight: in a matter of a few months, my husband (and sole income provider) lost his job, I birthed my second baby in less than two years, we had to sell our home because we could no longer afford it, and I decided it would also be a good time to jump into the entrepreneur-ial pool. Even though it's now been six years since that moment in time, I still get kinda queasy when I think about it.

Everyone, me and you included, has their breaking point—that messy, god-awful place where it's hard as hell to get back from. But I've found that right before that point, like an exit off the highway that's poorly marked and easy to miss, is this place where you get lit the fuck up and make the decision that nope, this isn't how this story is going to go, and you do something about it. Cory losing his job, and us having two kids under two, and selling my dream home back to back to back absolutely gave me emotional whiplash, but it didn't completely send me careening over the edge of my breaking point. Probably because, for me, I know the difference between downright difficult and severely inconvenient, and while I wouldn't wish my downright difficult on anyone, it's been the blessing in disguise that has guided me flawlessly for over fifteen years.

It's not comfortable to share the kinda sorta shitty parts of your life. I mean, I don't like to be a buzzkill, and I'd never want anyone to feel sorry for me, but it's not always sunshine and rainbows—you know that, right? Of course you do. Because I'm sure you've had your version of downright difficult, too.

Growing up, I knew my dad was sick. I knew he had a disease called myotonic muscular dystrophy, and I knew it meant his life was affected in different ways. As I got older, he had increasing trouble walking, talking, and performing basic life tasks. He was tired more often than not, and it sucked (that's not the downright difficult part).

You see, myotonic muscular dystrophy is a genetic disease that typically doesn't start affecting you until your fourth, fifth, and sixth decades of life. It's also a disease that can be much more severe if it's passed down from your mother (which, in my dad's case, it was). I remember growing up not knowing if I had this ticking time bomb sitting in my DNA, and it took up mental real estate in the form of me testing myself to see if my hands could squeeze things tightly, wondering if I looked more like my dad than my mom, and just an overall feeling of quiet dread.

When I met Cory, I quickly knew that he was the person I was going to marry, and before we went down the road of dating for years, getting married, and deciding to have children, I felt like it was the fair thing to do to see if I was, for a lack of better words, like my dad. It was a simple DNA test done at Georgetown University's MD clinic, and in the days that followed, as I waited for my results, I remember bargaining with God at an alarming rate. I would be kind. I would do whatever He wanted. I would stop complaining. I would save the motherfucking world, if *He* would spare *me*.

I got the call from Georgetown when I was back at school in my dorm room, and the doctor told me she'd like me to come in to discuss my results. The room did that thing again . . . it started spinning, and I didn't know if I was dying. It was hard to breathe, because I knew that if it was a "You don't have it," she'd have easily said that and we'd be on our merry way.

This meant I was like my dad.

I hung up with the doctor and immediately called my mom. As soon as she answered, a guttural cry came out of me, and it didn't stop for hours. It felt so unfair. So terrifying. So life-altering.

It's one thing to have a parent with a degenerative disease that has no treatment and no cure, but it's another thing to watch it unfold and know that it could very well be your future, too. That, like, majorly sucks and can be a complete mindfuck if I allow it to be.

So when people talk to me about business being hard, or social media being scary, or the unknowns of entrepreneurship being difficult to navigate, I understand . . . but I also understand that maybe they don't understand it like I do.

Maybe they don't understand that compared to a scary health diagnosis, social media is a walk in the fucking park.

Maybe they don't understand that, compared to helping your dad get dressed because he can't do it himself, business isn't that hard.

Maybe they don't understand that compared to the unknowns of an incurable, untreatable disease, the unknowns of business seem exciting.

Maybe they don't know that the power of a decision can change anything.

When I got my test results, I made the decision that I was going to be different from my dad. I was going to take care of myself in ways that he never did, and I was going to use science (pre-genetic diagnosis and IVF) to have healthy children so they wouldn't have to go through any of what I did.

I have three beautiful, happy, healthy boys. And as I sit here today, I have no symptoms of muscular dystrophy (which I celebrate the fuck out of, because my dad first became symptomatic at around twenty years old). I know that a diagnosis is not a definition or a death sentence, and I choose to live that way in both my personal and professional lives.

I'm not saying that you have to get some super shitty news to be this resilient, badass boss bitch like me (cue the sarcasm font again), but you do need to check yourself before you wreck yourself. Yes, being on video is scary and intimidating and just plain weird sometimes, but

I'm willing to bet that you've done things that are far scarier, far more intimidating, and much weirder than hopping on video to talk about a product you like using.

And life, much like social media, is ever-changing. As soon as you feel like you've got it under control, a curveball will be thrown, and you'll have to readjust your swing. That's why it's critical to maintain an authentic essence on social media, because although trends and algorithms may change, the fundamentals of human connection won't (yes, even as we enter the low-key terrifying world of all things AI, your personality will continue to act as a powerful magnet to your ideal clients).

IT'S SAFE TO BE YOURSELF

What if being yourself is a concept that feels genuinely foreign to you? I was being interviewed by my friend Shauna Van Bogart in her private membership community and we were discussing this idea of confidence and showing up as your authentic self, and I was saying how easy it is for me, when she asked me a question that turned my perception of this topic on its head.

"Did you grow up in a house where you felt safe being yourself?"

I was almost confused by the question. Of course that's how I grew up. While I didn't grow up in a family with extra money, we had an abundance of love and safety and happiness (which, I've learned, is oftentimes more valuable than money). Not only in my immediate family but in my extended family as well. Growing up with my brother and my cousins being my best friends, and my aunts and uncles feeling like second parents,

I never once felt the need to be anyone other than myself. As a child, my parents pumped me full of confidence that, looking back, was absolutely unwarranted. Truly, it was as if I had fallen from the awkward tree and hit every damn branch on the way down, but they never let me know it. As an adult, I remember looking through old pictures with my dad, and we came across some pictures from my middle school years. "You really were kind of homely," he said, "but I never once thought that at the time." I let it slide that my own father called me *homely* because the sentiment was there. I've always felt confident being *me*.

When Shauna asked me that question, it was a lightbulb moment. Even with my background in psychology and a master's in mental health counseling, I never thought about how so many of us fear being seen because it's always felt unsafe.

It reminded me of my friend Devin, who is an extremely successful business owner. She once asked if she could hire me to help her with Instagram. I laughed it off. "What could you possibly need help with?" I asked. She told me that it felt impossible to be herself on social media. I had noticed it, of course, but not in a negative way. I knew her in a professional capacity and as a friend, and those were two different sides of her. But so what? She told me, "You're you on social media, and that's why people buy from you. I don't make sales on social media because my audience can feel the gap between the professional me and the real me."

She was right. What you see of me on social media *is me*. If you were to meet me in real life, there would be no difference between the person you see on your phone and the socially awkward person standing in front of you. "Whether my audience knows that or not, they can *feel* it. *So just be you,*" I told her, almost flippantly.

But after digging deeper into this with Devin, I realized that she, like so many other people, grew up in environments where being herself never felt fully safe. She had to adjust her personality based on the mood her dad might be in, or she felt the pressure to maintain the perfect persona on the outside, based on the turmoil that was happening on the inside at her home that no one could know about. There was the burden of making good grades, rather than actually enjoying learning or being at school. She lived under the unspoken condition that to be loved and accepted, and to maintain a certain level of peace in her home, she had to *be perfect*. This is the kind of experience that doesn't leave you after you move out and start your life as an adult, no matter how much success you acquire along the way. There is so much healing and forgiveness that needs to happen for you to finally feel *safe* being yourself.

While we certainly can't do all that work together within the pages of this book, I want to remind you that *you are enough*. You don't need to be any other version of yourself than who you are at this exact moment in time. You are worthy and interesting and deserving and capable of receiving all the good in the world that's meant for you (unless, of course, you're an asshole or something). You have what it takes to create the safety and acceptance you've been seeking for so long.

HERE'S THE PART WHERE YOU ACTUALLY DO SOMETHING

You didn't think I'd share my downright difficult thing and not make you do the same, did you? Oh good, I didn't think so. Go on, you know the drill at this point; grab a journal or your phone or write with me here in the pages of the book, but it's time to get into your feelings.

- **What about showing up on social media feels scary or uncomfortable?**

- **What's something downright difficult in your life that you've survived?**

- **When you compare the scary, uncomfortable thing to your down-right difficult thing, what comes to mind?**

Let me guess: you're much braver than you've given yourself credit for.

Chapter 11

THE CONSISTENCY CALCULATION

After spending the last seven years working with entrepreneurially spirited humans, I've learned that one of the biggest challenges for people in their businesses is consistency. It's easy to be consistent when the money is rolling in, new followers are flooding into your account, and creativity is at an all-time high. But when no one is clapping for you, and the business that you're trying to get off the ground weighs a metric fuck-ton, it's more challenging to show up consistently.

People often feel overwhelmed because the world of social media moves so quickly. One minute it's posts, the next minute it's Reels, then it's TikTok or some trending audio that you need to keep up with. It can easily feel like *a lot*. But what's the one thing that matters more than the algorithm? You being *you*. When you can consistently and comfortably be yourself, you can effortlessly apply that knowledge to an in-person meeting or whatever social media app is currently the "it" channel. *You* transcend whatever medium you're choosing to use to connect with people. Being on social media is also the new equivalent of having a neon "open" sign hanging out in front of a brick-and-mortar store. If people don't know when to expect you, they'll go find what they're looking for somewhere else. I was reminded of this exact thing just last week when I went to get my nails done. The salon I typically go to opens at 10 a.m., but when I showed up at 10:45 a.m., and the open sign wasn't on (and the door was locked), I got in my car and headed to another nail salon. Few of us are out here selling something that people can't find a version of somewhere else. You're not the only coach, skincare expert, supplement distributor, or real estate agent out there, and the person who's ready to buy will not wait for you.

The other thing you do when you're inconsistent is build awareness for the business owner who *is* consistent. If you're a life coach and you inconsistently talk about the benefits of having a life coach, you're just planting seeds in your audience's mind that "life coaches are a good idea," and when they're ready to hire someone, they're going to go to the first person they think of when "life coach" comes to mind. It's *not* going to be you. It's going to be the coach, real estate agent, influencer, etc., who shows up consistently.

A common frustration for many people is that they feel like they *are* being consistent, but their sales and overall business growth are lackluster at best. If that tracks for you, I need to ask: are you consistently showing up on social media, or are you consistently engaging with your audience? Because those are two *completely different* things. For example, I could *consistently* go out and stand on a street corner and yell "I sell Unicorn Tears!" for three minutes straight, and then walk back inside feeling confused as to why not one person seemed interested in what I was selling. Or, I could *consistently* go out on the same street corner and set up a table with my Unicorn Tears on display, but more importantly, put a bowl of water out for the people who are walking their dogs, or lemonade, or a sign that said, "Tell me your favorite type of candy . . ." *whatever*. My point is, I'd be consistently going out there and engaging with the people who were around me. I'd be able to get to know their dogs' names, I'd create small talk and rapport, and people would come to expect that I'd be out there every day with some water for their dogs or a smile for them.

> Are you consistently showing up on social media, or are you consistently engaging with your audience? Because those are two *completely different* things.

Oftentimes, it's not the consistency piece that people get wrong—it's the fact that they don't know how to engage with the people around them, and for most people, knowing how to interact with people on the internet feels as odd as a two-dollar bill.

It feels odd (and, oftentimes, uncomfortable) because when you're interacting with someone face-to-face in "real life," you don't have time to edit what just came out of your mouth, and you certainly don't have the ability to watch (i.e., critique) *how* you're interacting with said person. Face-to-face, you're focused on the other person, but when you're creating content for social media, you're able to get distracted by angles and lighting, and you're focused on *you*, rather than the content and value that you're able to bring to the table. Being face-to-face, in person, feels natural, while talking to a camera with no one on the other side feels foreign as hell. What I'm going to do in this chapter is give you a tangible lesson in human interaction online. Remember, this is where the discipline piece comes in. You can read this chapter and think, *That's cool*, or you can read this chapter and *actually apply it*.

When it comes to working for yourself, there's a fine line between giving yourself grace and making an excuse. Tough pill, I know, but here's the thing I see all the time: one "bad day" sidetracks people for way more than a day. Picture this: it's the beginning of a new month, and you have high hopes about what you're going to accomplish. Your motivation (paired with discipline, of course) is through the roof, and you've got goals to crush.

But then you walk into your living room only to find that your cat, Gus, swallowed a rock and has had explosive diarrhea all over your living room. You not only have to rush to clean up the mess, but you also have to pack your kids' lunch boxes, get them to school, and make Gus an emergency vet appointment across town, all in a matter of twenty minutes. Because the morning was so chaotic, you forgot that one kid had to be picked up early for an eye doctor appointment, you forgot to take the chicken out of the freezer for dinner, and you were flustered as hell all day. You didn't even think about showing up in your business today because, well, *shit happens*. The thing is, this one frazzled morning bleeds into the days and weeks ahead, and by the time you're at the twenty-fifth of the month, you realize sales aren't what you'd hoped they'd be, so one of two things happens. You might sigh and concede that *the month is almost over, so I'll "be better" next month*, or you might turn into a sales chihuahua with commission breath, barking and peeing with excitement on anyone who looks your way, trying to sell, sell, sell. Neither scenario is a good one, and they're both absolutely avoidable when you make consistency a non-negotiable in your business.

You're allowed to have shitty, stressful days that sidetrack you and keep you from showing up in your full capacity. That's *life*. But you have to have the systems and discipline in place so that even when Gus is an idiot and swallows rocks, your one day of being unengaged in your business doesn't turn into a *month* of you being unengaged in your business.

Okay, that's cute, Colleen, but what if I have taken a month . . . or two . . . or three off? How do I hop back into it? Great question: I'm glad you asked. So maybe life has been crazy, and your social media presence is giving off *recently joined witness protection* vibes, and you feel like it's impossible to jump back in and start making connections *and* sales. I get it. The thing I *don't* want you to do is feel the need to make a grand reentry to your channel of choice. Think of social media as a big cocktail party. Say you're at this party, having a good time, chattin' it up with everyone, when you quickly excuse yourself to go to the restroom. "I'll be back in just a sec," you say. Your *intention* was to pop on in there, quickly pee, and head back to the party. But *oh no*, you're realizing that the spicy mini crab cakes that were being passed around as an appetizer (which you shoveled into your mouth with reckless abandon) are not agreeing with you, and your "quick" bathroom break has turned into a twenty-minute exorcism of your bowels. While you're sitting there alone, praying to your God and regretting your mini crab cake life choices, you start to fret: *I'm taking so long. Everyone's going to know that I'm pooping. PEOPLE CAN'T KNOW THAT I POOP!* Eventually, the exorcism ends, and you're able to regain your composure and reenter the party. As you do, you notice that everyone is still talking, laughing, and carrying on without any consideration as to how long you've been gone. They're too busy and too involved with their own situations. Assuming you're even somewhat socially aware, you don't find your group, barge into the conversation, and announce, "I'm sorry I was gone for longer than I expected. I thought I just needed to pee, but it turns out I had to take an emergency dump. It was touch and go there for a minute, but I'm okay now. . . . So, guys, what'd I miss?!"

Of course you don't do that. Because no one gives a shit (pun intended) about how long you were gone; you're just going to rejoin the group, smile and nod, and ease back into the conversation.

Social media is no different.

Maybe you *were* gone longer than you intended, because life and lack of discipline happen to all of us from time to time. Instead of making a dramatic return to social media, giving everyone the rundown of the drama and trauma, just pick back up where you left off. I can assure you, no one was making a note of how long it had been since you left. So breathe a little easier, my friend; you can do this.

Now that we've got that out of the way, we're going to turn a new leaf and start taking our consistency on social media more seriously.

In the following section, I'm going to walk you through what I call the *Consistency Calculation*. It's a two-week-long process that not only gives you examples of *what* to talk about on social media but also *how* and *why*. I could easily just give you two weeks of content and post ideas, but if you don't learn why you're doing it, you're not learning—you're simply parroting. My hope for you is that this section of the book helps you to start showing up in a way that builds genuine engagement and rapport with your audience. Yes, your stats and insights may very well improve, but so will your confidence and ability to create content that clicks with your unique audience.

HERE'S THE PART WHERE YOU ACTUALLY DO SOMETHING

Before we jump into the details of my sought-after Consistency Calculation, let's talk about your *current* relationship with consistency. Get out your journal or the note-taking app on your phone and consider these prompts:

If you were the most consistent version of yourself right now, what would your day look like?

_____

_____

_____

_____

_____

_____

_____

_____

_____

_____

_____

If you were the most consistent version of yourself, what habits of your current self would you be forced to change?

What's one area of your business that would most benefit from your consistency? What would the outcome of your consistency be?

Consider writing a journal entry as your most consistent self in the present tense. I always enjoy the exercise of writing about my goals as if they've already been accomplished, and I focus a great deal on describing the *feeling* of all of it! (Remember, our brains can't tell a real memory from a fake one, so get freaking excited!)

THE
CONSISTENCY
CALCULATION

DAY 1

STORY 1:

Share a piece of content that made you FEEL something.

Take a look through your saved Reels/posts from other content creators and find one with some substance/message.

FOR EXAMPLE:

> I shared a Reel from @victoriabrowne about Photoshop in videos. I typed up some text below the Reel saying how impactful it was to my mental health to see a beautiful, smart, UN-photoshopped woman on my IG feed.

> I got so much engagement from that and had wonderful conversations (a.k.a. MADE CONNECTIONS) in my DMs all day.

STORY 2:

Shout out someone who recently made your day/someone you're thankful for and say why.

This can be a video of you talking or a photo with text (tagging said person in either scenario). By doing this, you're a) making someone else's day, and b) the person may very well share it to their Stories (a.k.a. PUT YOU IN FRONT OF THEIR NET-WORKS).

Now, don't go tagging your favorite influencer, who you don't know, in hopes of them sharing it to their Stories. That's stupid and icky.

By saying why they made your day/why you're grateful for this person, it peels back a layer of YOUR onion for your audience, and they get to see a glimpse into your life/day/situation.

FOR EXAMPLE:

> I shared a photo of the monitor in my toddler's room at night with my husband sitting by his bed. I said how grateful I am that my husband has done the sleep training for all three kids. I got so many DMs about sleep training, sleepless toddlers/babies, husbands, and a lotttt of comments that led to content for the FOLLOWING DAY (in other words, your content creates content!!).

THE POINT: It's not about flashing your product or talking about your crazy month end; it's about just being you, sharing two simple snapshots into your life/brain, and inviting conversation to flow.

Your connections will be made in the conversations you're having in your DMs.

*Note: It is NOT the "strategy" to turn any of these conversations into business/product conversations! Just be a freaking human and trust the damn process.

DAY 2

Before we get to today's content here, stop and ask yourself: did any of your posts yesterday create conversations that could turn into content today?

FOR EXAMPLE:

> When I posted about my husband's sleep training, I got SO MANY DMs about how empty my son's room is! That wasn't the point AT ALL, and I would have never anticipated it . . . but I carried the conversation into the following day. I got on video and talked about the DMs I was getting, and then I put up a poll asking if people with toddlers had toys in their kids' rooms.

And, as no surprise to me . . . people had LOTS of opinions about it (I had tons of people in my DMs all day!).

If no one DM'd you yesterday, fret not! Here's what we're going to talk about today:

STORY 1:

Get on video and give a seemingly pointless opinion.

If you need help coming up with one, just pay attention to what's going on in your life today! Remember: when it's genuine and authentic to YOU, it will resonate!

FOR EXAMPLE:

> I got on video and talked about how I was so over my summer wardrobe and was ready for sweater weather. I didn't put up a poll; I just made a statement. Guess what? People shared their agreement (or disagreement: "I love summer clothes!!") with me all day!

STORY 2:

Did anything funny/stupid/annoying happen to you so far today? Share it.

Did you forget to switch the clothes from the washer to the dryer overnight? Did you spill coffee on your shirt? Did your kid/partner/pet do or say something ridiculous? You get the idea.

FOR EXAMPLE:

> "A few hours after sharing my pointless opinion about my wardrobe, I went out with my kids, and my five-year-old didn't have shoes. WTF?!"

STORY 3:

An ask

Here's where you're going to ask for referrals without being weird. You're going to literally say, "Okay, I have an ask for you—help me out. . . ."

FOR EXAMPLE:

> Say something like, "I was just talking to a customer of mine who's been using Unicorn Tears for a while, and they've really helped with her (fill in the blank). If you know anyone who has trouble sleeping/has anxiety/has fine lines and wrinkles/hates going to the nail salon/is fumbling their way through their health journey . . . send them my Instagram or put me in touch with them."

STORY 4:

Share a LIGHTHOUSE meme.

A lighthouse post (meme, Reel, etc.) is one that shares an actual opinion of yours, or it's on a topic you're passionate about. It's not vanilla, and it will not resonate with everyone (and that's the point).

It's a lighthouse post because it acts as a lighthouse for YOUR PEOPLE. It shines a light on who YOU are, so that YOUR PEOPLE can find you.

FOR EXAMPLE:

> I ended this hodgepodge day of conversation by sharing a post about LGBTQ rights. It's an important topic to me.

Dig in: what topics are important to you?

THE POINT: you're showing how you're a normal, multifaceted human with different things going on (even just in your head!) in one day.

Do you also notice how we follow up our ask with a lighthouse? Even though the lighthouse post (Story) has nothing to do with our business or the previous Story, it has a point. We're asking for referrals, and then not shying away from shining our light so our people can find us.

DAY 3

How did yesterday go? My hope is that it felt fun and natural, but the reality is that it may have felt difficult and awkward. (Both are equally fine and valid!)

Before you dive into the content here for today, ask yourself these questions: *Did anything come up yesterday in my DMs that I could use to continue (or start) a conversation? Do I want to know more about a topic I DM'd a few people about?* (Create a poll.) *Did I have any "ah-ha" moments while talking to people?*

Remember, our consistent content creates consistent content.

Ready to tackle day 3? Let's go.

STORY 1:

Share a Reel.

Yep, that's it.

STORY 2:

Share a product you use (from your product offering).

Here's the tip: BE COOL. And not like, "too cool for school" cool . . . just be a human. No need to freak out and tell everyone why it's LIFE-CHANGING and the BEST THING EVER. Just . . . mention it.

FOR EXAMPLE:

I sell CBD, and I normally take these CBD gummies before I leave to go pick my kids up from school, so that I don't end up with sensory overload when they tell/ask me 537 things on the car ride home.

So, when I would **<u>naturally use my product</u>**, I'll hop on Stories and say something like, "Can't forget my mom chill pill before I go do carpool pick up. Seriously, I would typically get so overwhelmed and snappy with my kids going a million miles a minute when they get home from school, and with these, that DOESN'T happen. Any other moms who struggle with sensory overload? You need these." (Add link.)

That opens my DMs in a way that says, "If you're like me, this is a safe space," and that's what people need to feel connected to you and want to buy what you're selling.

THE POINT: You showed up today. Congratulations.

DAY 4

STORY 1:

Offer a BTS glimpse of your family life.

Let me be clear: "family" does not have to mean the person you're married to, your 2.5 kids, and a white picket fence.

It can mean you and your cat.

The purpose of this is to show people what your life looks like outside of JUST you.

Who are YOU in relation to other people around you?

FOR EXAMPLE:

I shared a video clip of me riding in the passenger seat of my husband's Jeep with the doors off. There's nothing mind-blowing about that, but it got hearts racing, and even some people were saying, "I love my Jeep!" or "I've always wanted a Jeep!" or were even asking questions like, "Are you driving downtown?!" Whatever.

STORY 2:

Provide a snapshot of a happy moment from your day.

No, this is not creating a fake, curated Highlight situation. It just shows your network what made you happy today.

FOR EXAMPLE:

Starbucks? Having a picnic with your kids? Watching TV with your favorite beverage? Share it.

STORY 3:

Share a Reel that you can pair with a poll.

This can be funny, educational, heartwarming, anything! You're posting it because you found it to be of some value and you want to talk to our audience about it.

FOR EXAMPLE:

I shared a silly Reel a girl made about making the mistake of wearing her "standing" jeans to a "sitting" place. It made me laugh, and I posted a poll with it that said, "OMG, who knows the difference between standing jeans and sitting jeans?" (Answers: "Absolutely," and "WTF are you talking about?")

Of course I got just poll answers, but I also got a fair amount of DMs about it, too!

THE POINT: YOU ARE A HUMAN. You have a life. Things make you happy. And maybe some of the things from your human life will resonate with the human lives of the people watching.

And ending the day with a Reel and a poll will help boost your overall engagement for the day!

DAY 5

Today is going to be about upping the engagement with your audience and getting to know them better.

Think of today like being at a party or a happy hour . . . you're with people you may or may not know, and you're going to make small talk, but you're not so boring as to talk about the weather or divisive enough to talk about religion or politics.

Enter: pointless opinions.

These quickly start a conversation that gets people invested in a safe way . . . light enough that no one is ACTUALLY getting heated over these opinions, but relatable enough that people want to chime in.

What's a silly, mundane, yet everyone-has-an-opinion-about-this question you could ask your network today?

This will work best if you can tie it to your personal life experience or opinion (i.e., based on a conversation you recently had). When you're able to tie it up with a story, it always makes more sense.

But in case you need some help getting the juices flowing:

- Does the toilet paper roll over or under? There is only one right answer.

- PB&J sandwiches: equal parts peanut butter and jelly, more PB than J, more J than PB? (poll)

- When it's cold, would you sleep with socks on? (poll)

- Do you use a top sheet on your bed? (poll)

- Thoughts on decorating for Christmas before Thanksgiving? (poll or question box)

- It's taco night: what goes on the perfect taco? (question box)

- Worst Halloween candy? (question box)

You get the point, right? It's not serious, but it gets people to engage and pay attention.

If you find that you're getting lots of responses to a question box or that your poll is voting largely one way, hop on video and talk about it. You might say something like, "Oh man, who knew that people felt so passionately about Almond Joys being trash?" (I love Almond Joys, btw.)

THE POINT: HAVE FUN!

DAY 6

How'd your poll or question box go?!

These types of posts are so crucial to getting to know your audience and buildiang a relationship with them.

FOR EXAMPLE:

> Like I mentioned earlier, over on my personal Instagram account (@colleen__nichols), I do something every week called Question Box Sunday.

I ask pretty wild questions, and get equally wild answers, and it's a way that I've built SUPREME trust with my audience.

I don't think most people here will end up asking QBS-type questions, but I know that having question box/poll content in regular rotation not only helps with engagement but also helps you get to know the people who have their eyeballs on you.

So now that we have eyeballs on you, let's talk about a few things today.

STORY 1:

If applicable, do a quick video updating/wrapping up the question box. Any major themes/takeaways?

STORY 2:

Share your product.

> Do your best to weave it into the question box from yesterday (if that's totally awkward and not possible, don't worry about it! Just share!)

FOR EXAMPLE:

> "I'm so stressed out from those of you who don't use a top sheet that I'm taking a little extra CBD today, good golly. And yes, this is a friendly reminder that if we have any other stressed-out, nervous nellies in the crowd, you need to buy these damn jellies. I don't know if it'll help the no-top-sheetin' psychopaths, but it's worth a shot." (Add link.)

What I'm doing here is a) using humor, and b) reminding people of what my product HELPS with . . . without sounding like a weird infomercial. And guess what? People pay attention.

STORY 3:

Share a lighthouse Reel or meme.

Share a product/business and then make sure people know who you are.

FOR EXAMPLE:

> I shared a Reel about women's rights and added the text "HELL YES."

> Easy peasy lemon squeezy.

STORY 4:

Do a callback/update.

What did you talk about earlier in the week that you can update everyone on?

FOR EXAMPLE:

I had shared about my toddler's lack of sleep situation earlier in the week and got enough engagement from that to signal to me that this was a topic I could come back to (PAY ATTENTION to what your audience ends up talking to you about). So I got on video and did a "We're still sleepless in Seattle" solidarity post.

By doing this, we're creating a sense of community and closeness. We're bringing people into the fold and keeping them updated on a life situation.

LET ME BE CLEAR:

The situation that you can update people on does NOT have to be serious. Remember the chick who gave updates about how many socks her son left on the floor that day? I follow someone else who gives periodic updates about his neighbor's grass. It doesn't have to be deep to create a sense of camaraderie.

STORY 5:

Share a funny meme.

When you're scrolling on your phone at night and see something funny, share it. Sharing things that you find funny helps people learn your sense of humor, which is super important in relationship building.

THE POINT: Any time you do something that gets a lot of engagement one day, leverage it the next. You will almost always see me selling something the morning after Question Box Sunday.

DAY 7

STORY 1:

Make a recommendation about a product/good/service you DO NOT sell.

Being seen as a resource for solid, helpful recommendations is vital to your success, so it's massively important that you're giving them regularly.

What's the last thing you bought on Amazon?

Are you in a program or working with a new coach that you love?

What's the thing on Netflix that everyone (who likes the same thing as you) needs to watch?

Now, don't go making a recommendation willy-nilly just to make one. Really think about this because, remember, we're building trust here. If you recommend something that you don't LOVE, people won't feel inclined to try, buy, or watch it.

STORY 2:

Share one of your favorite accounts that you follow.

Tell your audience WHO needs to follow them and WHY. Sell it to them.

FOR EXAMPLE:

I shared a post from Shauna Van Bogart. I said, "If you're in business or are a human being who likes to receive good things from the Universe, you MUST be following Shauna. Period. End of statement."

Of course, tag whoever you're recommending. Is it a given that they will reshare to their Stories? No. But it can't hurt.

THE POINT: Your recommendation matters. If people end up liking the shorts from Amazon and like that account you told them to follow, they're more likely to pay attention when you mention the Unicorn Tears they need to buy.

DAY 8

STORY 1:

Ask for a recommendation.

What's something that you're currently in the market for (be it a good or a service) that you could absolutely Google and find the answer to? ASK YOUR AUDIENCE.

FOR EXAMPLE:

I was in the market for a pair of jean shorts. Yes, I Googled and spent time on Like to Know It, but I wanted to have a conversation about it with the people who spend time watching my Stories.

This helps you in two ways:

1. You can end up sharing the most suggested brands/links/whatever because people WANT to know. Why? They, too, are looking for recommendations!

2. You'll be able to use this as content at a later date.

FOR EXAMPLE:

I ended up buying three pairs of shorts that were recommended and was able to do a "try on" in my Stories, showing everyone what worked and what didn't, and I was able to provide them with links.

Doing this will help you find something you're genuinely looking for, and it sets you up to be a helpful resource to your network.

STORY 2:

Share a funny meme or Reel.

Never underestimate the power of weaving humor into your personal brand, content, and business. We want our audience to see US first and our business second.

STORY 3:

Share your favorite product in one minute or less.

We're not going to drone on and on about our "life-changing hero product" and bore our network to tears. Instead, we're going to QUICKLY pop in and tell people what the product is, who it's for, and why they need it.

FOR EXAMPLE:

"My mind has been going a million miles a minute today, so I'm taking a CBD gummy before bed to calm me the hell down. If anyone else out there feels like they have trouble turning their brain off at night, you need this." (Add link.)

THE POINT: We're starting our day by generating engagement by asking people to share their opinion about something they love. They're talking to us, we're talking to them, and the algorithm keeps showing your stuff to people.

And because there are potentially more eyes than normal in your Stories today, you're going to quickly mention your product. It's also strategic because you've extended an olive branch by trusting them (individuals in our audience) for their recommendation, so they're more inclined to trust your recommendation to them.

It's a back-and-forth.

And a give-and-take.

It's natural.

DAY 9

STORY 1:

Post a screenshot of social proof.

Social proof sells, and we're here to sell. You want to show your audience that other people are loving the things that you sell.

FOR EXAMPLE:

> I took a screenshot of a customer's DM telling me how much my Unicorn Tears were helping her and making a real difference. I shared that, then added my link saying, "Get them here."

> Now, if you're thinking, *But wait, I don't have anyone in my DMs telling me how much they love my Unicorn Tears!* . . . then go create it.

> How? Send a text or DM to one or two of your best (or kindest) customers, saying, "Hey, Sarah! I wanted to get some feedback on the Unicorn Tears—how are you liking them?" or "Sarah, I know you've been a customer for six months—what would you say to someone who's considering buying Unicorn Tears?"

> They'll respond.

> You'll have social proof.

> And your customer will be doing the selling for you today.

STORY 2:

Share an embarrassing story.

People bond over embarrassing stories. Embarrassing stories disarm people, and oftentimes, they make people laugh. Now, this doesn't have to be a TRAUMATIC embarrassing story—you choose your comfort level—but show your "not perfect" side.

FOR EXAMPLE:

I shared how I had just gone to a Starbucks drive-through and it was so awkward when I was ordering, and I was embarrassed. I ordered my regular Grande Decaf Vanilla Latte (don't come for me, caffeine fiends; that shit makes my heart beat way too fast), and the barista asked, "Hot or iced?" Friend, the way "hot" came out of my mouth sounded like I was trying to make this man my sugar daddy. It was one of those moments where I don't know if he heard it like I did, so I didn't want to draw attention to it by saying something like, "Sorry for that random sultry voice at 7:45 this morning." But *I* knew what it sounded like, and I was mortified. So, of course, I had to tell my Instagram friends about it. It was silly, but it got people laughing and sharing similar stories.

That's the win—you're getting other people to tell you about THEM.

STORY 3:

Post a funny meme or Reel.

Bonus points if it can tie into your embarrassing story from earlier.

FOR EXAMPLE:

> I had shared the previous story about being awkward, and then later in the day I shared a meme about being socially awkward. It made us feel like we were now in on a joke together.

THE POINT: Yes, you're selling today, but more than that, you're being a HUMAN.

Remember, when we're selling, we want to show our audience the type of person we are so they feel a sense of connection to us (and, in turn, are more likely to buy from us when the time is right for them).

DAY 10

STORY 1:

Share a lighthouse Reel/meme/post.

We've talked about our business two days in a row, so it's time to turn up the brightness of your lighthouse, my friends.

FOR EXAMPLE:

> I shared a post that a company I buy from was donating funds to an organization that I align with and also support. Not everyone agrees with said organization, but that's okay!

> I don't share these things simply to be divisive—they are important to me, and I never want a customer to be surprised about who I am as a person. That's a shitty feeling that I think we have all been able to relate to at some point.

> Having trouble figuring out your "lighthouse" content? It's usually the stuff that you'd *want* to say but are afraid people will judge you (for whatever reason!).

> ***Note: This is not just about politics or religion—far, far from it! And it does NOT have to be divisive. It is simply meant to shine a light on topics, issues, causes, etc. that YOU care about (<u>for example</u>: workload stress on healthcare professionals, teachers' salaries, climate change, low-tox living, etc.).**

STORY 2:

Give a recommendation.

It's our job to earn the trust of our network, and we do that by talking about things we do NOT personally sell/earn commission on.

FOR EXAMPLE:

> I shared a new-to-me brand of decaf iced coffee that I've been drinking for a few weeks and really enjoy. I shared the company, why I like it, and who needs it.

STORY 3:

Share a BTS look at your day.

This can be a video or a picture, but the point is to simply show an "un-highlight reel" part of your day that your network can relate to in some way.

FOR EXAMPLE:

> It had been A DAY. You know the kind . . . where nothing actually terrible went wrong, but it was a million micro-inconveniences that just freaking added up. I posted a Story about it being 4:00 p.m., my kids were in front of the TV, and I was going to serve them frozen pizza for dinner because I was just D O N E.

People normally just show the "successful" parts of their day, and while there's nothing wrong with that, it's vanilla; it's beige; it lacks substance. It also doesn't warrant a ton of conversation. It's easy and nice to watch, sure, but it's not much to talk about.

Lastly, we want to show our networks behind the scenes as much as possible because it shows them that if we can do this business while being busy, imperfect humans . . . they can, too.

THE POINT: You're showing up as YOU today, my friends. What do you care about, what do you recommend, and what does your life look like if we peek behind the veil? You're the person people connect with, want to talk to, and eventually want to buy from/join in business.

DAY 11

STORY 1:

Ask an opinion about FOOD.

What's something we ALL do? EAT.

And man, oh man, do people love to talk about food.

As we discussed in Direct Sales Growth Community recently, asking a question about food strikes up SO much engagement. This can be a poll or a question box, but it has to be cued up authentically (meaning, tie it back to a conversation you recently had . . . which ALL of you can reference Office Hour!)

FOR EXAMPLE:

> Get on Stories and say something like, "I was on a call the other day, and someone was talking about how she doesn't eat the skin on salmon, but her partner does. And this sparked up MANY a heated opinion, which got me thinking about how I love peanut butter and chocolate, but my husband thinks it's disgusting (he's obviously a psychopath, duh). So tell me, what's your unpopular food opinion?"

If you do a question box, share some of the answers throughout the day, and then do a "yum/yuck" poll and have people engage that way!

Remember: There's none of this "Boo-hoo, no one answered my question box." Answer it yourself if you need to!

THE POINT: This is to show you that you don't need to post content through the day to create a ton of conversation and engagement. This is to teach you that if you ask the right questions, the conversations will flow!

DAY 12

STORY 1:

Wrap up the food conversation.

FOR EXAMPLE:

> "Thanks for weighing in on the food conversation yesterday. Now I'll never look at salmon without thinking of you guys ever again."

By doing that, we're creating a community . . . an inside joke . . . camaraderie . . . something to "call back" to later on.

STORY 2:

Give an opinion about your business (or product—whatever your focus is!).

FOR EXAMPLE:

> Say something like, "Since we're on the topic of opinions, I have one about money—it's fun to have more of it than you need."

Poll: agree/disagree.

STORY 3:

Tie in the business.

FOR EXAMPLE:

> A network marketer could say something like, "PS—to all of you who agree that it's fun to have more money than you

need ... you know what I do with (company name), right? Right. For those of you who want to make more of it (without having to go get a second in-person job), slide into my DMs and we'll see IF this might be a good fit for you."

STORY 4:

Share a lighthouse meme/Reel/post.

FOR EXAMPLE:

I shared a Reel about LGBTQ youth and their parents.

Again, you're not here to do business with just anyone. You're here to do business with YOUR people. Don't dim your light in hopes of trying to appeal to the masses—shine it so the right ones find you.

THE POINT: You're learning to tie your content together so that it feels like a story, and when you bring up the business (or product), it doesn't feel discombobulated and out of left field.

You're also leaning into your CONFIDENCE. There is so much power in knowing that you're not for everyone; you're just showing up for your people. You belong. You're in the right place. There's no need to try to be anything other than yourself.

DAY 13

STORY 1:

Go on a mini rant.

When I say "rant," I simply mean give your unfiltered, real-life take on something that's happening in your life at the moment.

FOR EXAMPLE:

I had shared a meme/infographic about the toxins in Halloween candy, and then I got on my Stories and said something to the effect of, "Apparently all Halloween candy is killing our children, and there's no fun left in anything, and I hate it here, and I'm just freaking overwhelmed by all of it. WHY IS IT SO HARD TO BE A MOM?!"

Again, yours doesn't need any negative connotations. Maybe you're talking about how you're overwhelmed by the beauty of nature. I don't know. Whatever it is, though, it MUST be authentic and leave the door open for conversation. This was just a real-life moment that I had, and it garnered a ton of conversation.

STORY 2:

Share something related to your mini rant.

FOR EXAMPLE:

I shared a post from a dietitian who gave some good ideas about simple swaps for Halloween candy that were REALISTIC. And I said something like, "I love how she gives real life suggestions—and not just organic dark chocolate that costs $23 for a 4-pack."

I'm continuing the conversation, while also acting as a recommendation resource by sharing another account that was helpful for me.

STORY 3:

Ask people for their recommendations regarding the mini rant topic.

FOR EXAMPLE:

I said something along the lines of, "Let's pretend none of the candy is killing us; what's the one Halloween candy you can't turn down?" (question box)

*Share results as they come in and do a "yum/yuck" poll, or later share the most popular answers and do a poll to vote for the favorite.

STORY 4:

Resolve the rant.

FOR EXAMPLE:

I said something like, "Listen, it's hard to make decisions as a parent in today's world. Whether you hand out toothbrushes and carrots or gum and Skittles, we're all just doing our best, you know? Will I have an Almond Joy on Halloween? Probably. Will I let my kids get a sugar

rush on Halloween? Probably. But that's not our NOR-
MAL, so I feel okay about it."

THE POINT: Today is an example of having a real-time conversation with your audience and getting to know them and
improving your engagement levels!

DAY 14

STORY 1:

Give a recommendation about something you LOVE but <u>do not</u> sell.

What is something you use every day (or frequently enough) that you feel like everyone needs in their life?

FOR EXAMPLE:

> I have something called a BedJet. It's like an AC and/
> or heater for your bed. It's AMAZING, and I love it so
> much. I showed people what it looked like, how I use it,
> and why I love it. And, of course, I share a link and tag
> the company.

STORY 2:

Share a product that you love and DO sell.

Notice the energy you were in when you made the last Story. It didn't feel weird, and you were confident. This is no different, okay? You're simply in recommendation mode, so keep the ball rolling.

FOR EXAMPLE:

> A few hours later, it was time for me to take my daily
> CBD gummy, so I documented it. I talked about why
> I take it (it calms my anxiety and overstimulation as
> a mom to three young, very loud, very hyper boys),

and I said that if anyone can relate to that (being over-stimulated), they need these things ASAP. Of course, I added my link. (I do not feel it necessary to tag the company here.)

STORY 3:

Give a glimpse into your day, and low-key tie in your product.

This can be a video or a picture with text.

FOR EXAMPLE:

I was unloading the dishwasher, and all three kids were within twelve inches of me. I snapped a pic and added text along the lines of, "5,500 square feet, and it means nothing to these Velcro children. This is where they are, always. I love them dearly, and also, can you see why I love my CBD. #nopersonalspace."

Here, my post was 95 percent focused on ME and my day, but it also served as a call back to my previous Story and gave a real-life example of why I love my product. It's also something that people can respond to and engage with, regardless of whether they talk to me about CBD.

STORY 4:

Share something that made you laugh.

This can be your own content or something funny from somewhere else.

FOR EXAMPLE:

I shared a funny Reel from a comedian I follow. Easy peasy.

THE POINT: You're selling today, but it should feel easy and natural! We start the day by "selling" something that we don't *actually* sell, and we're proving to ourselves that, yep! selling IS easy and natural, and we do it all the damn time. From that same energetic space, we then show up and sell something from our own product offering. And guess what? When you show up in the right energy, people notice.

DAY 15

STORY 1:

Ask for a recommendation.

This can be about ANYTHING, but of course we want to make it specific and easy for your audience to answer. The less they have to think about it, the more likely they are to engage.

FOR EXAMPLE:

We WON'T say, "What's the best thing you've ever bought on Amazon?" because that requires them to think about all the purchases they've ever made. It's too large of a mental category for them to sift through in a matter of seconds.

Instead, we'll ask something more specific (and give a backstory as to why we're asking for this recommendation), like, "I'm in the market for a new concealer—do you have a brand that you love?" (question box)

Assuming it's within reason, take a second to shoot over a "Thank you, I'm going to check this one out!!" DM just to let them know you appreciate their recommendation.

If there is an overwhelmingly repeated recommendation, make sure to share it with the group! Like, "It sounds like Shape Tape is the #1 recommendation so BRB I'm going to Ulta."

STORY 2:

Ask about weekend plans.

FOR EXAMPLE:

> Instead of asking "What's everyone doing this weekend?"
> you're going to give them some insight into what YOU
> like doing on the weekends, and then give them a poll.

FOR EXAMPLE:

> I'm no longer twenty-three, and Fridays aren't a party.
> They're for putting my kids to bed and sitting on the
> couch with takeout and Netflix. LITERAL Netflix and
> Chill. No one touch me. Let me eat and zone out and
> go to bed.

Then I'll ask my audience, "What's your ideal Friday?" (Poll:
stay in and be a couch human/go out and do something fun)

Often, when I give options with no middle ground, people
will end up in my DMs telling me things like "Both! I like to do
something fun but be home by 8 p.m. and watch Netflix!"

So I get people responding to my engagement sticker AND I
have people in my DMs . . . win-win!

STORY 3:

Based on your Friday plans (stay in vs. go out), ask for an appropriate recommendation.

FOR EXAMPLE:

> I told everyone I'm staying in and watching Netflix. So I'm going to say, "Okay, we have T-minus 4 hours before the clock strikes 7 p.m. and I can turn into a potato. What are you currently watching (or have you just watched) and love?"

As always, that evening or the following day, I'll share the most popular responses and what I ended up choosing.

THE POINT: We are making friends today. We are asking them for their opinions and input because they MATTER. The more you can get to know about your audience (Do they spend lots of money on makeup or not? Are they party animals or homebodies? Do they like true crime docs or rom-coms?), the more value you can add in the coming days, weeks, months, etc. This is LITERALLY like making a friend IRL.

The more you know about them, the more the relationship can blossom.

And when that relationship blossoms, they know, like, and trust you.

And when they know, like, and trust you, they buy from you.

Do you feel like you're getting the hang of this whole "don't make it weird" thing? When you think of social media like a virtual party that you get to flitter about and have fun conversations with interesting people, rather than an awkward chore that makes you feel dumb, your conversations will turn into conversions, and you'll be one happy human.

The point of this consistency calculation exercise is to show you that you can, in fact, be a human on the internet. While I refer to this as the Consistency *Calculation*, it's more of an art form than anything else, and it's one that you're absolutely capable of mastering. Again, this is one of those things that I can lead you to, but I cannot execute for you; you *have* to take the initiative and *actually* do it. Yeah, it might feel awkward and uncomfortable, but do you know what else feels awkward and uncomfortable? Being a stagnant entrepreneur.

Remember that, over time, when your content is killer, your confidence burns like a bonfire, and you're consistent as fuck, sales *will* start happening.

ONE LAST THING...

The fact that we've both made it to the end of this book is mind-blowing to me, but here we are. As we've walked through the process of digging through your fears and the bullshit stories you tell yourself, and we've identified the way you actually want to show up on social media—like a real human who is messy and imperfect but takes massive action—it feels fitting to admit that I don't even know how to end a book. I literally just sat on the floor of my office reading the endings of some of the books that changed my life, hoping to draw some inspiration from people who know what they're doing (or at least faked it and fooled me). I'm also not a fan of goodbyes—in fact, I'm the master of the Irish exit. I simply slip out the door so I don't have to hug anyone and get stuck in the inevitable loop of new conversations that could have been had earlier in the evening, because now I'm just ready to go home, put on my soft clothes, and sit on my couch alone scrolling TikTok for an hour before it's time to go to bed.

The thing is, you already have all the answers when it comes to being yourself and connecting with people. To make an impact on social media, you have to keep in mind that you're not trying to be for everyone; you're trying to be for the *right* ones. When you get stuck in the trap of being focused on following trends rather than following your gut, that is when things start to get weird. The trends and apps and channels are going to be ever-changing, and the way to pierce through all that bullshit is by simply being unapologetically yourself. Sales and business growth become a natural byproduct when you act as a lighthouse for people. Believe me when I tell you that right now, this very second, there are people out there scrolling the interwebs looking for *your* brand of messy imperfection. They're looking for *your* story, *your* sense of humor, and *your* value. There are absolutely people out there who are already selling, writing, and creating offerings that are similar to yours, but that doesn't matter. There are currently just shy of five b-b-billion people who use social media today, so you better start believing that there is enough room for what you bring to the damn table, and people are hungry to consume it. The secret ingredient is *you*.

There's a Judy Garland quote that's become a mantra for me in my personal and professional lives, and it's this: "Always be a first-rate version of yourself, instead of a second-rate version of someone else."

You're not here to try to emulate someone else, or to be a version of yourself that you think is more palatable to the consumer. One last example for the road: I think ranch dressing is fucking foul, but that doesn't stop ranch dressing from being her ranchy self for the people who absolutely *adore* her and put her on everything (I'm gagging).

Whenever I say the fuck word on the internet, someone cringes. Some people even take it to the next level and send me a DM or email saying, "Some people don't like that kind of language, Colleen." To which I respond, "Yeah, but some people *love it*." It then blows her mind that I would risk offending some people who are lukewarm towards me in order to appeal to the ones who are piping hot, but that's exactly what you have to do to stand out amid the noise.

As someone who wants to create an irresistible attraction between you and your audience, you don't have the luxury of having the personality of a wet rag. Remember, you're here to be a bonfire, surrounded by countless people who love the environment you're creating.

Not everyone will love you, want to consume your content, or buy whatever it is that you're selling, but when you're unabashedly yourself, the *right ones* will become superfans—and none of it will feel weird.

ACKNOWLEDGMENTS

My Mommy—It would be impossible to thank you for everything you've done for me, but I'll say it anyway. I admire you, love you, and thank God every day that He paired us up. Thank you, thank you, thank you.

Cory—You are the best man I've ever known, and I am eternally grateful that we both ended up at that fraternity party my first weekend of college. You are everything to me. Thank you for believing in me when I don't believe in myself, and for encouraging all (okay, most) of my crazy ideas. I like you, I love you, and I will always choose you.

Jack, Oliver, and Cooper—You are forever and always the first things I thank the Universe for. Thank you for reminding me that none of this work stuff actually matters, because at the end of the day, none of it impresses you. You know me as your butt-wiper, snack tray maker, boo boo kisser, and bedtime song maker upper and I love it more than anything.

Brian—My first friend, and my favorite brother. You are all the good and fun and joy that I've ever wished I could be. Thank you for always being the absolute best person I know. I'm so fortunate to be your sister. I love you.

Mark and Joni—Thank you not only for raising my favorite human, but for being such an invaluable support system. This book, and my business, wouldn't exist if we didn't have your support. From Willpage, to being the best Grammy and Pop the boys could ask for, and everything in between, thank you. I love you both! And Joni, thanks for the green bra!

Emily—Thank you for being my very best friend and being the one person I've never once had to pretend to be anyone other than myself around. (I guess when the ER is one of your first hang outs, that helps.) Thank you for always helping me make things pretty, for cheering me on without fail, and being my person. I love you!

Shauna—Thank you for being one of my dearest, closest friends. I adore you, am inspired by you, and being your friend is one of the easiest things I've ever done. Asking you to write the forward was a complete no-brainer, and I cannot thank you enough. When you're the next Oprah, I'll gladly be your Gayle.

Megan—I have to give credit where credit is due, and Cory being Team Megan Kjolsing from the jump is one of his smartest predictions to date. I could not be more thankful for the presence you have in my life and in my business. You are kind, compassionate, smart, and I can trust that you will always tell me what I need to hear, not what I want to hear. DSGC could not be what it is without you, and I will be forever grateful for what you've done for me. Thank you for being such a wonderful friend!

Natalia & Erin— Thank you for everything you've done for me. You have the kindest way of telling me that what I'm creating isn't cute, and I appreciate it more than you know. Thank you for taking on the rebrand of No Shame Sales Game and for changing the trajectory of the cover of this book. Most importantly, thank you for being friends who I trust, brainstorm with, and can send "WTF" texts to without fear of judgment.

To my OG IG friends—I would not and could not be where I am today without you. Thank you for virtually hanging out with me and embracing me being a human on the internet.

To my blog readers— You were the first humans who planted the idea in my head (many years ago!) that maybe I could string words together in a way that connects people. Thank you, thank you.

To past, current, and future DSGC members—Thank you, thank you, a million times, thank you. I am endlessly grateful that you've allowed me to operate in your orbits.

Jen Sincero—*You Are a Badass* changed the trajectory of my life and it gave me the belief that I could succeed in ways that previously seemed impossible.

Tyler Spring—Thank you for sending me the most serendipitous DM asking if I'd ever considered writing a book. No one knew I had just finished my first draft the day before. Thank you for guiding me through my first book writing journey!

Mariah Swift—Thank you for making this book writing process feel so easy. Your calm energy is so magnetic. Maybe after I'm a *New York Times* bestselling author, you'll accept my IG follow request.

Ash Abraham—Thank you for guiding me through the editing process and being the voice of reason that I so often needed. You were the first person to read my book in its entirety, and hearing your positive feedback meant the world to me!

The early readers—Thank you for being people who I trust and respect so very much. Your words, feedback, and encouragement have been appreciated more than you could possibly know.

To you—If you're holding my book in your hands, please know you are making my lifelong dream come true. I am mind blown that you and I exist in this scenario, and I couldn't be more grateful for you if I tried. Thank you, thank you, thank you. `

JOURNAL PROMPTS

You finished a book! Let's make sure you didn't just waste your time, mmkay? Here are 8 *extra* journal prompts to help get your social media humanness juices flowing.

1. We talked about sharing more authentically online about things you don't make a profit off of sharing about. What are 10 purchases you've made in the last 30 days that you've actually liked and can talk to your audience about (hopefully this book is one of them, omg)?

2. Think fast. Someone in an imaginary scenario just told you that you had to get on stage and talk about one thing, anything, for 10 minutes straight. What would you choose? Why?

3. What's a part of your true self that you hide from social media? Who would benefit from you sharing it?

4. Take a look at your current social media channel of choice. What are the first three words that come to mind? Are they aligned with who you are and what you want to accomplish?

5. Who are three accounts you love following on social media, and why do you enjoy their content?

6. Who are three people you follow on social media whose content you always scroll past, and why do you find it to be boring?

7. If someone followed you on social media and then met you in real life, what would they be surprised to learn about you?

8. Uh oh! You're at a family cookout when you've been cornered by Great Aunt Peggy, and she asks what you're doing for a living these days. How do you explain it?

Want to get in touch with me or learn more about social media marketing? Check out the QR code below.